New cinema in Eastern Europe

A surprising number of highly original films have emerged from
Eastern Europe—mainly from Poland, Hungary and Czechoslovakia, but also from Yugoslavia and Bulgaria—despite the
severe political pressures to which the nationalized cinema in this
part of the world has been subjected. In *New Cinema in Eastern
Europe*, Alistair Whyte concentrates on these countries, selecting
for examination directors who have succeeded in developing
their own individual talents—often despite the limitations of an
official socialist realist conception of art.

In Poland a new cinema began to develop in the late fifties
when Andrzej Wajda and Andrzej Munk gained international fame
with films such as *Ashes and Diamonds* and *Eroica*. Their works
are examined in depth, as are films by newer directors such as
Jerzy Skolimowski. The Hungarian cinema even in the fifties
produced films as worthwhile as Zoltán Fábri's *Professor Hannibal*,
but Western interest was really aroused by the discovery—through
The Round-up—of Miklós Jancsó, whose main themes and
formal elegance are here discussed with sensitive understanding.
It was the sixties that saw the emergence of a whole series of
films from Czechoslovakia: Jiří Menzel, with the whimsical,
bitter-sweet quality of *Closely Observed Trains* and *Capricious
Summer*, Miloš Forman, with his delicately observed portrayal of
everyday life in *A Blonde in Love* and *The Firemen's Ball*, are
among the directors discussed. The book also examines, from
Yugoslavia, Dušan Makavejev (*The Diary of a Switchboard
Operator*) and films from Bulgaria (including *The Peach Thief* by
Vulo Radev), Albania, Romania and East Germany. While concentrating on individual directors, the author has not overlooked
consideration of recurrent national themes.

Alistair Whyte is a lecturer at Westfield College, the University
of London.

D1708452

Eva Ras in Dušan Makavejev's *Love Dossier—Tragedy of a Switchboard Operator* (1967)

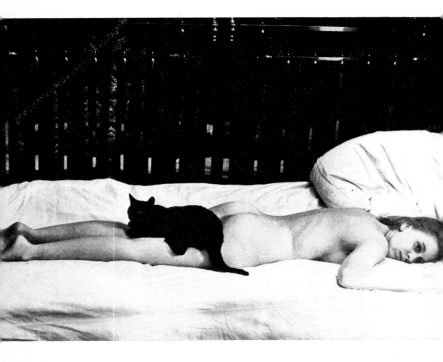

Alistair Whyte

New cinema in Eastern Europe

General editor David Herbert

Studio Vista | Dutton Pictureback

COVER ILLUSTRATIONS
Front cover Jiří Menzel in his *Capricious Summer* (1968)
Back cover Jan Nowicki, Joanna Szczerbic in Jerzy Skolimowski's
Barrier (1966)

© Alistair Whyte 1971
Designed by Gillian Greenwood
Published in Great Britain by Studio Vista Limited
Blue Star House, Highgate Hill, London N19
and in the USA by E. P. Dutton and Co., Inc.
201 Park Avenue South, New York, NY 10003
Set in 8D on 11 pt Univers
Made and printed in Great Britain by
Richard Clay (The Chaucer Press), Ltd, Bungay, Suffolk

SBN 289 70094 9 (paperback)
      289 70095 7 (hardback)

Contents

Introduction

For the purpose of this book the term Eastern Europe is taken as referring to those countries which have become communist, or, more correctly, socialist states since the end of the Second World War—that is Albania, Bulgaria, Czechoslovakia, the German Democratic Republic, Hungary, Poland, Romania and Yugoslavia.

In these countries the film industry is, of course, state-controlled and therefore runs the risk of being extremely vulnerable to political pressure. Indeed at various periods attempts have been made to map out rigid guidelines for artists in all fields: in 1949, for example, Polish film-makers were told to take part in the ideological struggle by portraying on the screen 'the positive hero of the new Poland'. Such an approach to the cinema is a form of 'socialist realism', a doctrine most forcefully expressed at the Pan-Soviet literary congress of 1934: introspection and interest in imaginative, stylistic devices is condemned, while portrayal of man in his everyday life and of the virtues of socialism is encouraged.

Nevertheless, the cinema has flourished in Eastern Europe, especially in the 1960s, and films from many of the countries concerned have gained critical acclaim throughout the world. For the most part, however, such works represent a rejection of the strict precepts of 'socialist realism'.

The aim of this book is not to serve as a history or as a comprehensive dictionary of Eastern European films since 1945, a rôle which is admirably filled by Nina Hibbins's *Eastern Europe* in the Screen series, but to examine the main features of this 'new cinema'. I shall therefore concentrate on certain countries and certain directors—those artists who by their choice and treatment of subject stand out not merely as skilled technicians but as individual creative film-makers.

7

Zbigniev Cybulski in Andrzej Wajda's *Ashes and Diamonds* (1958)

Poland

Polish films were among the first from Eastern Europe to be widely acclaimed in the West and Poland has produced not only Zbigniev Cybulski, the first socialist 'superstar', but also Roman Polanski, one of the few directors whose name is known to the cinema-going public at large.

The immediate postwar years saw the production of a limited number of films dealing with the occupation, the ghetto, the resistance and the destruction of Warsaw. As might be expected from the suffering undergone by Poland during the war years, these subjects are powerfully felt and they are still major themes or obsessions in present-day films. The two most impressive works of the period are Wanda Jacubowska's *The Last Stage* (1948) about Auschwitz and Aleksander Ford's portrayal of wartime youth, *That Others May Live.*

In 1949 an arid period began when film-makers were told to follow the doctrines of socialist realism, and for the next four years few films of any value were produced, except perhaps for Aleksander Ford's *Five Boys from Barska Street.* In 1954, however, things begin to change. Andrzej Wajda made his first feature *A Generation* and, at the September meeting of the Polish Association of Cinema and Theatre, Jerzy Toeplitz, director of the film school at Lódź, condemned the oversimplified works of recent years. The change in the political climate brought about a re-organization of the film industry into independent production groups. This was the beginning of the emergence of an exciting new cinema in Poland but before considering the younger directors who made their mark in this period a word must be said about the doyen of the Polish film industry, Aleksander Ford. His postwar films can still be viewed with pleasure. *That Others May Live* (1947) is an attempt to show the years 1939–43 by concentrating on the fortunes of five young people and their families. Inevitably the film is rather schematic but certain sequences such as those in the ghetto are brilliantly handled and the over-all visual elegance does somewhat compensate for the simplified

9

Tadeusz Janczar in Aleksander Ford's *Five Boys from Barska Street* (1953)

human relationships. In *Five Boys from Barska Street* (1953) Ford shows how five youths, on probation for theft, succeed in becoming useful members of society. Surprisingly, this film was attacked by the authorities for the choice of semi-criminals as heroes. Today the characters appear as cardboard figures but the film is exciting, especially in the final chase through the sewers, or in the 'soul-stirring' brick-laying sequence on the building-site. The

Aleksander Ford's *The Knights of the Teutonic
Order* (1960)

second scene does have a certain epic quality about it and it is
this quality that Ford exploits in his most famous film, *The
Knights of the Teutonic Order* (1960), which is an impressive
spectacular that enjoyed much success both at home and abroad.
Aleksander Ford is not a particularly original director but he does
succeed in creating interesting works within the limitations of a
format.

Andrzej Wajda's *A Generation* (1954) with (from right to left) Tadeusz Janczar, Urszula Modrzynska, Roman Polanski, Tadeusz Lomnicki

To find originality one must turn to those film-makers who made their debuts in the fifties. The most famous of these, Andrzej Wajda, worked as assistant director to Ford on *Five Boys from Barska Street* and his own first feature, *A Generation* (1954) does bear certain affinities with the earlier film. Wajda's protagonists, however, are much more convincing than those of Ford and less stylized than the typical positive hero of the socialist states at that time. 'We have all lived through occupation,' said Wajda in an interview with Boleslav Sulik, 'and it appeared to us much simpler, more ordinary, more normal. Those boys were around us, and no one was acting as a hero.' Heroism, conscious or unconscious, deep attachment to traditions or ideals to the extent of self-sacrifice, these themes deeply concern Andrzej Wajda and can be seen developing through his so-called trilogy, *A Generation,*

Zbigniev Cybulski, Tadeusz Lomnicki in Wajda's *A Generation*

Kanal, Ashes and Diamonds. The director's aim in *A Generation*
was to show that ordinary people were capable of acts of extreme
courage, but not only for ideological reasons. Stach, the leading
character in *A Generation*, moves from layabout to more positive
hero, but for a number of reasons, not the least being his love for
Dorota. And the famous last scene of the film stresses the hero's
personal tragedy by showing his grief at the arrest and inevitable
death of his beloved. As the actor who played Stach, Tadeusz
Lomnicki, himself pointed out, this was contrary to the ideas of
the time, for a hero did not have the right to weep but should
stoically face up to his destiny. Even more interesting than Stach
is the character Jasio, played by Tadeusz Janczar. Cowardly yet
capable of extreme violence, as is shown in the scene where he
shoots down a German officer, Jasio with all his doubts, hesitation

Wienczjslaw Glinski in Wajda's *Kanal* (1956)

and final defiant suicide can be seen as a prototype of the complex hero of *Ashes and Diamonds*. Perhaps this character was one of the features of *A Generation* which displeased the authorities, for the film was severely criticized and certain scenes were cut.

Wajda's next feature, *Kanal* (1956) was also attacked but the film enjoyed immense popularity at home and gained praise abroad, which made the Polish critics change their minds. The title refers to the Warsaw sewers where, after the unsuccessful uprising of September 1944, hundreds of fleeing soldiers died like rats. It is a grim and gripping film which makes an immediate impact on the emotions, yet it is ambiguous, reflecting, perhaps, the ambivalence of Wajda's own attitude towards war and heroism. There is a certain demythologizing of heroics as Wajda shows the deaths of his protagonists in all their horror, degradation and futility, but what is one to make of the end of the film? Having reached safety, the commander discovers that, as a result of the cowardice of his lieutenant, none of his platoon is with him. After shooting the man the commander goes back into the sewers, his face showing grim despair. This useless yet moving action illustrates the ambiguity of the film—the heroism is futile yet there is, to quote the critic in the *Spectator*, 'a message of underlying glory'.

Teresa Izewska in Wajda's *Kanal*

In *Ashes and Diamonds* (1958), Wajda's third film, the main protagonist, Maciek, impressively acted by Zbigniev Cybulski, is very much an anti-hero, especially in the context of a socialist society, for his mission is to shoot down a communist party official. He is a man who enjoys killing, as is shown in the violent assassination sequence at the beginning, a man who fights for sentimental rather than ideological reasons, as is illustrated by the famous bar scene where he lights vodka-filled glasses in memory of dead companions. But as the film progresses Maciek is shown growing to a new awareness, through love (as in *A Generation*), through realization of the hope reborn with the end of the war—out of the ashes may come diamonds. He is, however, unable to escape his past. 'He found himself in a situation with no way out,' said Wajda in an interview published in the French film review *Positif*, March 1966, 'carrying out the order given to him was to oppose the law of peace, and not carrying it out was opposed to the cruel laws of war. The two laws collided in Maciek's character. It is not without significance that the action takes place on the last day of the war and the first day of peace.' *Ashes and Diamonds* is constructed around the pull of contradictory forces—war/peace, death/life, tradition/reform. This raises the whole question of Wajda's style.

At one time an art student, Wadja reveals in all his films a feeling for sequences of great visual impact. *A Generation* has an impressive opening sequence constructed of a sweeping pan moving into a descending tracking shot which finally comes to rest on the hero Stach, playing a knife game with two friends. *Kanal* also opens with a tracking shot which relentlessly follows the platoon across a scarred landscape bombarded with shells. Wajda himself has stated that his films are made around certain images. In *Ashes and Diamonds* this feeling for the telling image develops into a form of symbolism, as for example in the sequence where, as Maciek supports in his arms the man he has just killed, a burst of fireworks, in celebration of the end of hostilities, illuminates the sky. Again, one of the most striking sequences is the *polonaise* danced at the end of the film ; this scene borrowed from a symbolic play by Wyspianski is full of references to self-indulgent

traditionalism. There is also Maciek's grotesque writhing death on an enormous heap of rubbish, showing how Wajda uses the external scene not only as a backcloth but also to punctuate, extend and intensify the drama he is portraying.

Wajda's next film, *Lotna* (1959), picks up many of the threads of the trilogy. Again the concern is with heroism, again Wajda's attitude is ambiguous, but in this colour film the director's romanticism is pushed farther than ever before. The title, meaning 'the swift one', refers to a white mare, owned successively by three members of a Polish cavalry troop during the disastrous 1939 September Campaign. A white mare is a Polish symbol of victory but here it takes on a deeper significance—referring to Poland itself and to tradition. The whole film is full of symbols

Zbigniev Cybulski in Wajda's *Ashes and Diamonds*

Jerzy Skolimowski, Tadeusz Lomnicki in Wajda's *Innocent Sorcerers* (1960)

and *leitmotifs* which are intended to create a work that is poetic rather than dramatic. And although it is difficult to overlook the weaknesses in the narrative, although the life/death symbolism is perhaps too heavy and the use of the pathetic fallacy too much in evidence, *Lotna,* especially in the exciting cavalry charge sequence, is a dazzling film to watch.

After *Lotna* Wajda turned to a contemporary subject. *Innocent Sorcerers* (1960) took a disenchanted look at contemporary youth. Jerzy Skolimowski, now one of the leading young Polish

Serge Moulin in Wajda's *Samson* (1961)

directors, was asked to collaborate on the script. The result is an extremely verbal film, an unsuccessful combination of the styles of two different film-makers.

With *Samson* (1961), Wajda returned to the war period: the film, which follows the fortunes of a Jew who escapes from the ghetto, is an attempt, not entirely successful, to rework the Biblical story of Samson. There are, however, some very powerful scenes, such as the opening sequence which shows the Germans boarding up the ghetto entrance.

Siberian Lady Macbeth (1962), made in Yugoslavia, is a melodramatic and uneven film—the confined drama of the first part unhappily married to the epic quality of the prisoners' trek across Siberia at the end. In 1962 Wajda contributed an episode to *Love at Twenty*. In this, Cybulski plays a war veteran who saves a child from an animal at the zoo. A young girl invites the man home, makes love to him; her friends arrive and get the 'hero' drunk, and he talks about his war experiences, which mean nothing to the mocking group of young people. Both in content—

Andrzej Wajda's *Siberian Lady Macbeth* (1962)

the theme of outdated bravery, of the war, of the past clashing with the present—and style—the sudden flashbacks to the war period—the episode in *Love at Twenty* is a 'crucial transitional work', as Colin McArthur pointed out in his excellent article on *Everything for Sale* (1968). This latter film, made after two historical features, *Ashes* (1965) and *Gates to Paradise* (1967), is in part a tribute to the actor Zbigniev Cybulski, Maciek in *Ashes and Diamonds*, who was killed in 1966 as he jumped off a train. It is, however, no Hollywood-type biography. Using a form

Barbara Lass, Zbigniev Cybulski in Wajda's *Love at Twenty* (1962)

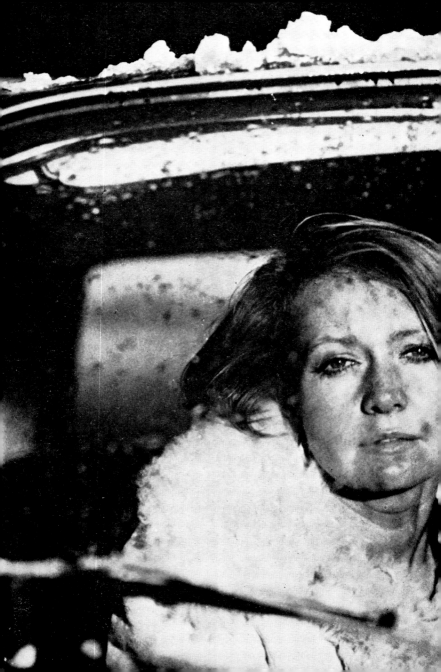

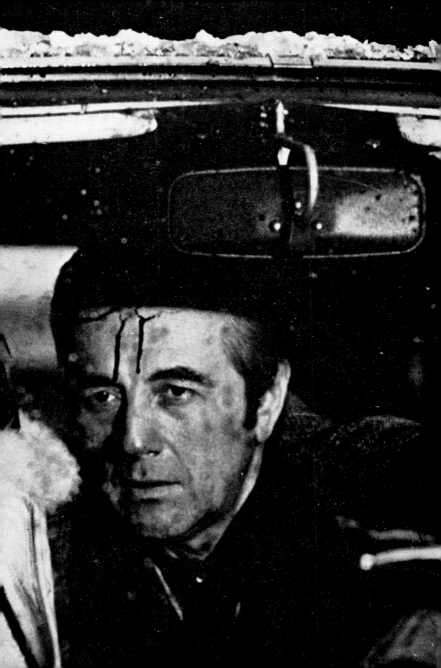

similar to that of André Gide in his novel about a novel, *The Counterfeiters,* Wajda has made a film about a director making a film entitled *Everything for Sale* which is transformed into a tribute to its leading actor when the latter dies as he jumps off a train. The result is very much a critical self-appraisal of Wajda himself. All the ambiguities of his attitude towards the war, heroism, tradition are clearly shown ; and the whole film is full of deliberate visual references to his cinematic universe, one of the most obvious being a pastiche of the bar scene with the burning vodka in *Ashes and Diamonds.* And through the semi-self-portrait of the director Wajda shows he is aware that the artist may appear unfeeling or even sadistic, since he observes, analyses and uses for his art personal crises and the most tragic events. This is evident in the scene where the director photographs his own bleeding forehead after a minor accident, or in the final sequences where the scene of the actor's death, with careful attention to the blood on the snow, is reconstructed for the purposes of the film within the film. This interrelation of art and reality is one of the major themes of *Everything for Sale* and there are sequences where the spectator is unsure whether he is watching the film or the film within the film : for example, one is shown an attempted suicide but the camera pulls back from the actress with her cut wrist to reveal a studio set.

The rich content and inventive technique of *Everything for Sale* re-established Andrzej Wajda as one of the most important contemporary directors. And after this work Wajda's *Hunting Flies* (1969) came somewhat as a disappointment, although it is visually impressive and marks another stage in the director's developing freedom of style. There is a certain amount of social satire of the contemporary scene in Poland—the discothèque in

on pages 24–5
Elzbieta Czyzewska, Andrzej Lapicki in Wajda's *Everything for Sale* (1968)

Elzbieta Czyzewska in Wajda's *Everything for Sale*

Warsaw, the snobbish artists' club—but above all *Hunting Flies* is a lightweight sex comedy with a Skolimowski-type hero played by Zygmunt Malanowicz—and a beautiful heroine, Malgorzata Braunek, who appears very much as the predator.

Landscape after a Battle (1970) is, however, as challenging and beautiful a work as *Everything for Sale*. The film shows the liberation of prisoners of war and their transfer to a camp for displaced persons. This is not, however, a 'realistic' film ; there is no attempt at a meticulous reconstruction of the period, the released prisoners of war do not seem under-fed and many scenes exist not as dramatic necessities but as examples of Wajda's concern for plastic beauty. The external scene is used to intensify emotion

◀ Zygmunt Malanowicz, Malgorzata Braunek in Wajda's *Hunting Flies* (1969)

Daniel Olbrychski in Wajda's *Landscape after a Battle* (1970)

Stanislawa Celinska, Daniel Olbrychski in Wajda's *Landscape after a Battle*

and mood: the camp is surrounded by black barren earth; the forest where the hero and heroine make love is beautiful but autumnal, hinting at the approaching death of the girl. At the same time *Landscape after a Battle* has a rich thematic content. Despite the immediately postwar setting the film can also be considered as an allegorical work referring to conditions in contemporary Poland and raising such problems as the rôle of the individual in society, compliance with rules for the sake of rules, blind attachment to abstract ideals. It is, however, not only a political or social allegory but also yet a further exploration of Wajda's preoccupation with life and death, past and present. As in *Everything for Sale*, the main protagonist is an artist, but here he is a poet and a far more tortured individual than the film director Andrzej. He detests the regimentation of the camp, which is a form of living death, yet he is afraid to leave. 'To live is to forget,' he says, but he himself seems unable to forget either

Kazimierz Opalinski in Andrzej Munk's *Man on the Track* (1956)

the past or his deep attachment to Poland and he cannot adjust to the present, to life as represented by the young Jewish girl.

Wajda's later works have become more introspective, more stylistically inventive, more complex in content, yet he is very much an *auteur* in that one can observe themes, images and attitudes recurring and developing in all his films from the out-wardly 'socialist realist' *A Generation* to the very imaginative *Landscape after a Battle.*

Andrzej Wajda's romanticism is often contrasted with the ironic approach of Andrzej Munk, whose first feature, *Man on the Track,* appeared in 1956. For this film Munk obviously drew on his experience as a maker of documentaries, especially *A Railwayman's Word.* The setting of the railway, the organization of the station is presented with what appears to be great authen-ticity but not in the socialist realist manner. Orzechowski, the old engine driver, is not the positive hero of the New Poland. He is a

Edward Dziewonski in Munk's *Eroica* (1957)

proud difficult man, hostile to change, severe towards his stokers. Although ultimately he does appear heroic he is not suddenly transformed but remains true to himself; it is the outside world which has almost wickedly misunderstood him. The character Orzechowski and the events leading up to his death are revealed through a series of personal memories and flashbacks, while the film opens and closes with the death of the man on the track, which gives it a cyclical structure.

Eroica (1957) won Munk great international fame. In this film in two episodes the controlled, unflamboyant style of *Man on the Track* develops into humorous distancing and irony. Dzidzius, the main protagonist of the first episode, which is set in Warsaw during the war, is the extreme opposite of the positive hero. The whole episode is satirical and very funny especially in such scenes as the one where Dzidzius, sitting drunk at the edge of a river, is

Josef Nowak, Tadeusz Lomnicki in Munk's *Eroica*

threatened by an enormous tank. In the second episode, set in a prisoner-of-war camp, the humour is absent but in its place is bitter irony. Munk is not so much concerned with the cruelty inflicted by the Germans on the captives, as with the tensions, hatreds and sufferings caused by the prisoners themselves: their pettiness is shown, as are the prejudices of certain imprisoned officers attached to conservative and authoritarian ideals. There are, however, brief moments of solidarity when the captives talk of Zawistowski, the one man who has apparently escaped. The bitter irony is that it is a myth that fosters this solidarity since Zawistowski did not escape but is hiding in the rafters of the prison hut. When ultimately he dies the three prisoners who know the truth arrange to smuggle his body out in order to keep the myth alive. This is a very sombre, unmelodramatic episode set for the most part in the *Huis Clos* atmosphere of the prison hut.

Bogumil Kobiela in Munk's *Bad Luck* (1960)

Munk's next film *Bad Luck* (1960) has not been so widely
shown in the West, despite prizes gained at Cannes and Edinburgh.
It is again an ironic work about a man who is very much an anti-
hero. In six flashbacks it illustrates episodes in the life of Jan
Piszczyk who always followed popular trends but always the
wrong ones. Despite its satire and humour *Bad Luck* becomes
rather repetitive.

In 1961 Munk was killed in a car crash. The film he was making,
Passenger, was unfinished but the director's friend and colleague
Witold Lesiewicz assembled the fragments already shot. The film
is built around a confrontation on a boat, fifteen years after the
war, of Liza, who had been an officer in a concentration camp, and
Marta, a prisoner with whom Liza had had a special relationship.
This would have led to a series of flashbacks to the concentration
camp, building up a picture of the complex relationship between
captor and captive, torturer and victim, and attempting to understand how a man or woman can be an accomplice to such crimes.
While the sequences on the boat were not filmed and are evoked

through stills, most of the concentration camp sequences were completed. These are extremely effective, showing, in a matter-of-fact way, how something as appalling as the gassing of women and children can become an almost routine daily event. It is of course difficult to pass any real judgement on this incomplete work but these fragments hint at what could have been a fascinating, important film.

Aleksandra Slaska in Munk's *Passenger* (1961)

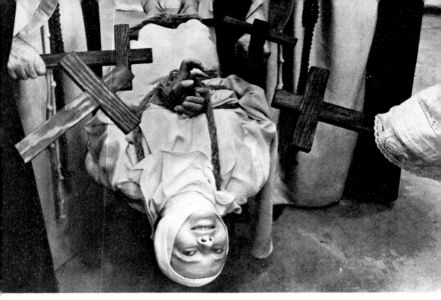

Lucyna Winnicka in Jerzy Kawalerowicz's *Mother Joan of the Angels* (1961)

Another director who attracted much attention in the late fifties and early sixties was Jerzy Kawalerowicz whose best-known film, *Mother Joan of the Angels* (1961), was awarded the special jury prize at Cannes. Set in the eastern plains of Poland in the seventeenth century, this work is concerned with the attempt to exorcise the demons apparently possessing the mother superior of a remote convent. Yet Kawalerowicz is not wishing to explore demonology but to examine and, as he said himself, protest against 'the external restrictions placed on man whether these are Catholic or not'. In a crucial central scene the exorcist goes to ask a local rabbi for advice but the rabbi is shown to be just as helpless as the priest. (The same actor plays both rôles.) All that the rabbi can offer is a suggestion that the mother superior is not possessed by demons but that it is merely her human nature

Kawalerowicz's *Mother Joan of the Angels*

asserting itself. Her 'possession' is thus a form of madness born of the strain between her desire to be a saint and her human nature. For the same reasons, the misguided beliefs of the priest, who is 'possessed' by his very human love for Mother Joan, lead him to slaughter two innocent people, in the belief that, by this crime, he will take all the guilt on himself and thereby allow Mother Joan to become a saint. Kawalerowicz is a self-declared atheist but his film is not a piece of crude anti-religious propaganda, it is a work of art which illustrates very subtly, within a historical context, the disastrous results of a blind faith which is opposed to the drives in man. All this is perhaps *too* subtly presented, for the formal beauty of *Mother Joan of the Angels,* the white-clad nuns contrasting with the black surplice of the priest, tends to detract from the human problems at the core of the film.

In 1964 Kawalerowicz began work on the very expensive film *Pharaoh* (completed 1966) which has had distribution problems in the West. This is extremely impressive as a spectacle but at the same time Kawalerowicz has attempted to deal with serious issues. The problem of power, the struggle between tradition and reform, are treated with a complexity that is unusual in a film of such dimensions.

Tadeusz Konwicki, who worked on the scripts of *Pharaoh* and *Mother Joan of the Angels*, himself directed an interesting feature film *The Last Day of Summer* (1958). Set on a lonely beach, with jet planes occasionally zooming across the sky, the film deals with a man and a woman who are both scarred by the past. Although the film is interesting as an experiment, its poetic quality and the meaningful shots become extremely irritating.

Kawalerowicz's *Pharaoh* (1966) ▶

on pages 40–1
Jan Machulski, Irena Laskowski in Tadeusz Konwicki's *Last Day of Summer* (1958)

Barbara Kraftówna in Wojciech Has's *How to be Loved* (1962)

Wojciech Has also began to make films in the fifties but it is his work of the sixties that is better known abroad. In *How To Be Loved* (1962) Zbigniev Cybulski plays a weak character, certainly not a positive hero, a narcissistic, mediocre actor forced to hide in the flat of a girl who loves him. Their relationship is revealed in a series of flashbacks as the girl, now a mature woman, remembers the past during a flight to Paris. She gradually strikes up an acquaintance with the man next to her who, at the beginning of the film, appears quite dull and unfeeling. Thus while in the

Zbigniev Cybulski, Barbara Kraftówna in Has's *The Saragossa Manuscript* (1964)

flashbacks the story moves to a sad ending, the suicide of the actor, the present tense of the film does offer a certain growing hope. For the most part the films of Has deal with weak characters and are tinged with melancholy, but in 1964 he turned to a very different subject, *The Saragossa Manuscript*. Adapted from a novel written in French but by a Pole, this is a tale of the fantastic tinged with wild black humour. Amusingly directed, incredibly complex and starring a plump Cybulski, *The Saragossa Manuscript* is perhaps Has's best film to date.

The late fifties and early sixties thus saw the emergence of an impressive group of directors who broke away from the restrictions of socialist realism to create a number of original and very varied works. Indeed almost every Polish film of this period merits attention, but the mid-sixties marked a decline. One could point out a certain number of reasonably amusing works which are interesting for their disrespectful attitude towards bureaucracy and to the war—for example *An Italian in Warsaw* (1964) by Stanislaw Lenartowicz, which takes an irreverent swipe at the war and the Polish resistance, with an incredibly exaggerated performance by Cybulski as the artist wishing to avoid taking sides. This period also saw the first features of two fascinating young directors— Roman Polanski and Jerzy Skolimowski.

These two, together with Walerian Borowczyk, raise certain problems in the context of a study of cinema in Eastern Europe, for all have worked in the West. Since Borowczyk's only live-action feature to date, *Goto, Island of Love*, was made in France, it cannot be included. Skolimowski has not left Poland altogether and the features he has made abroad are very much in line with his Polish films. Polanski, unlike the other two, seems to have severed all links with Poland. He went back from France to make his first feature, *Knife in the Water*, and since then all his films have been made in the West. Thus, despite the brilliance of such films as *Cul-de-sac* and their importance for the student of Polanski, this book will concentrate on his early shorts and his first feature.

Polanski was born in Paris of Polish parents in 1933. He began acting at the age of fourteen and appeared in many of the films of the fifties, including *A Generation* and *Lotna*. He helped Wajda to prepare the sound effects on *Kanal* and worked with Munk on *Bad Luck*. While at the Lódź film school he made a number of extremely distinctive shorts, the most famous of these being *Two Men and a Wardrobe* (1958). Polanski described this strange, disturbing film in the following terms:

Two men come out of the sea carrying a wardrobe and go into a town, i.e. into life. But because of this wardrobe they cannot benefit from life. By this I want to show a society which rejects the human being who does not conform or who is, in its eyes, afflicted by some moral or physical defect. And on all sides, in the town, terrible things are happening, cruel things, but no one sees them or wishes to see them. (Interview in *Positif* No. 33)

In *Le Gros et le Maigre,* a short made in France in 1961, Polanski shifts to an examination of the relationship between individuals. In this picture of the cruel exploitation of the thin man by the fat man there is humour but it is very sick humour. The atmosphere is reminiscent of the world of Samuel Beckett: the situation of the two men echoes the complex relationship between Lucky and Pozzo in *Waiting for Godot.* The struggle between two isolated individuals entirely dependent on each other is also the theme of the short *Mammals* (1962). Two characters in a snowy landscape fight and argue over the right to sit on a sledge and be pulled.

Zbigniev Cybulski in Stanislaw Lenartowicz's *An Italian in Warsaw* (1964)

Jolanta Umecka, Zygmunt Malanowicz in Roman Polanski's *Knife in the Water* (1962)

Zygmunt Malanowicz, Leon Niemczyk in Polanski's *Knife in the Water*

The conflict of individuals in a close relationship is the major theme of Polanski's first feature *Knife in the Water*. A successful sportswriter and his wife pick up a hitch-hiker and they eventually invite him to spend the week-end with them on their yacht. The film portrays the resultant complex tensions. Polanski himself has stated that 'the young boy is just an excuse; the conflict is between the couple'. It is, of course, true that the older man is trying to prove something to his wife, nevertheless the struggle between the two men takes up most of the action. Typical of Polanski are the sado-masochistic elements in this struggle and the repeated reminders, especially through the knife which the young man is constantly handling, that violence could erupt at any moment. It must not be forgotten, however, that this film was co-scripted by Skolimowski and does bear some of his trademarks—concern with material objects, with cars, and so on. Indeed *Knife in the Water* has been described as something of a hybrid.

on pages 50–1
Skolimowski in his *Rysopis*

After *Knife in the Water* Polanski made three films in England *Repulsion, Cul-de-sac, Dance of the Vampires* (an American co-production) and in the USA *Rosemary's Baby*. The most successful of these was *Rosemary's Baby* but the most impressive, and incidentally, the film of which the director is proudest, was *Cul-de-sac*, a brilliant black comedy with echoes of the absurd.

In the films of Polanski there would appear to be two recurrent situations. On the one hand, he is concerned with the sufferings inflicted on the outsider by a society which overlooks its own inconsistencies and brutalities—*Two Men and a Wardrobe* and, to some extent, *Repulsion*; on the other with the conflict of individuals thrown into a dependant relationship—*Mammals, Knife in the Water, Cul-de-sac*. In both cases the individuals are shown to be cut off in some way from the outside world or society, yet in both cases he is not just commenting on exceptional circumstances, but presenting his rather pessimistic vision of life. There is in all Polanski's work an apparent fascination with cruelty and violence.

Slightly younger than Polanski, Jerzy Skolimowski began as a writer. After collaborating on the script of *Innocent Sorcerers* he became a student at the Lódź film school and in 1960–61 collaborated with Polanski on the script of *Knife in the Water*. Skolimowski's own first feature, *Rysopis—Identification Marks None* (1964), was made over the years he was a student. Consequently the film has a rather loose structure and is somewhat episodic. It portrays ten hours or so in the day of a young man waiting to leave for his military service. The hero, Andrzej Leszczyc, is constantly on the move, meeting old friends, talking to his mistress, encountering two other women (all three are played by Elzbieta Czyzewska, Skolimowski's first wife), dealing with officials. He is an outsider, dissatisfied with his way of life, seeking something but he does not quite know what. All this is apparent in the film as a whole but especially in the scene where Andrzej is interviewed and expresses his desire to travel, to drive through Poland. (This may remind one of Godard but Skolimowski claimed that, at the time of *Rysopis,* he had not seen any of the French director's films.) There is also criticism of the society

Skolimowski in his *Walkover* (1965)

from which Andrzej is shown to be alienated—most obvious in the sequence where he is interviewed by the draft board, but implicit in the film as a whole.

In *Walkover* (1965) the hero is once again Andrzej Lesczczyc and once again Skolimowski himself plays the part. The film, however, has a much more professional look about it and the hero is seen to be much more consciously trying to prove himself as an individual. He wins his first match in the boxing competition at the factory where he works but knows that he will be unable to

Jan Nowicki, Joanna Szczerbic in Skolimowski's *Barrier* (1966)

beat his next opponent. He leaves with his girl-friend but finally decides to return. The boxing in the film takes on a deeper significance for it illustrates the hero's inability to take the easy way out; and his instinct to fight, although he knows he will lose, can be construed as a form of rebellion. The irony is that he is awarded the title since his strong opponent Wielgosz scratches from the tournament. Yet the final image is one of defeat since Wielgosz finally does appear and after a dispute about the prize knocks Andrzej to the floor. *Walkover* casts a disillusioned eye on contemporary Poland and the factory background allows social and political comment to be introduced.

The picture of contemporary Poland that emerges from Skolimowski's next feature, *Barrier* (1966), is even more critical of existing social structures. The title refers to the lack of communication between the young and the old, between the establishment and the non-conformist. The hero is once again a student drop-out but Skolimowski himself no longer plays the rôle and the film is far more stylized than *Rysopis* or *Walkover*. It is an amusing yet menacing fantasy where everything seems to have a symbolic quality, for example, the strange sequence in the café which is suddenly filled with war veterans wearing paper hats and singing patriotic songs. This refers to one of the main barriers between the generations—the war. Skolimowski speaks for the young Poles who associate the war not with their own experiences—as does Wajda—but with the traditionalism of their parents. Yet despite the pessimistic picture of society, Skolimowski does suggest the possibility of a positive relationship between his non-conformist hero and his tram-driving heroine. *Barrier* is a bizarre, fascinating film full of striking images, even if it does give the impression that the director is trying too hard to be poetic—a criticism levelled against it by Roman Polanski.

Le Départ (1967) was made in Belgium with two actors used by Godard—Jean-Pierre Léaud and Catherine Duport. Although highly inventive it is not a complex fantasy like *Barrier*; and it is a much funnier film. The hero is a young hairdresser who will do anything to obtain a Porsche in order to drive in a rally. Skolimowski's own ambiguous attitude to luxury objects is evident, for although the hero's interest in cars is meant to represent a false set of values, the manoeuvres of the Porsche are filmed with loving attention. Ultimately the young hairdresser decides not to race but to stay with the girl. Thus, like *Barrier*, this film ends with the hope of a fruitful human relationship.

Jean-Pierre Léaud in Skolimowski's *Le Départ* (1967)

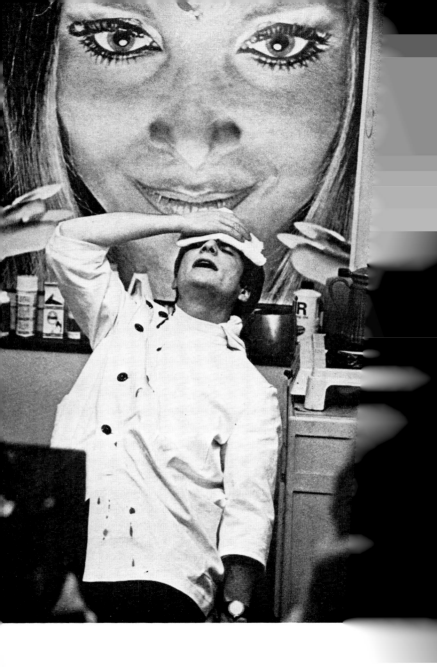

Skolimowski's *Hands Up!* (1967)

After *Le Départ* Skolimowski returned to Poland to make *Hands Up!* which continued the story of his hero, Andrzej Leszczyc. This is, he himself says, his 'best and most mature film, and it is not funny at all'. Unfortunately *Hands Up!* was banned by the Polish authorities but in 1970 Skolimowski made some alterations to the film which will perhaps lead to its release.

Skolimowski's next two features were made in the West. *The Adventures of Gerard* (1970) is an attempted parody of the epic adventure film with tinges of black comedy. It is, however, a very strained work with which Skolimowski himself is said to be dissatisfied. *Deep End* (1970), also made in English, is more in line with the earlier films. The hero is an adolescent who has left school to work in a swimming pool. The film shows his growing sexual awareness and his love for the experienced young woman

Daniel Olbrychski in Jerzy Hoffman's *Colonel Wolodyjowski* (1969)

attendant, admirably played by Jane Asher. Their relationship, however, is far from fruitful, for the girl is totally unpredictable and capable of being wilfully cruel. *Deep End* is often extremely funny but a disturbing note creeps in which culminates in violence. The film ends with an extraordinary scene of the boy, under water in the pool, clasping the naked body of the dead girl as the blood streams from her mouth. The violence of this image, the humour elsewhere in the film, the episodic quality of the narrative, are typical features of Skolimowski's works, but *Deep End* lacks the wider social implications of his Polish films.

In Poland itself the most successful film of 1969–70 was Jerzy Hoffmann's *Colonel Wolodyjowski*—an extremely costly epic in the style of Ford's *Knights of the Teutonic Order.* The hero is played by an ageing Tadeusz Lomnicki with stiff-upper-lip courage,

Jadwiga Chojnacka in Stanislaw Lenartowicz's *The Red and Gold* (1969)

Andrzej Zarnecki, Jan Mislowicz in Krysztof Zanussi's *Structure of Crystals* (1969)

except for the odd nervous twitch. The villain, who, ironically, is the most revolutionary character in the film, is portrayed by the ubiquitous Daniel Olbrychski, since the death of Cybulski the leading Polish actor. Although the human relationships are ludicrously oversimplified, there is some compensation in the splendid battle sequences at the end of the film.

In the field of comedy at the end of the sixties, there was *The Red and Gold*, a charming feature by Stanislaw Lenartowicz who made *An Italian in Warsaw*. A middle-aged woman believes herself to be a widow but a man turns up claiming to be her long-lost husband. *The Red and Gold* is extremely funny and tender without ever becoming over-sentimental. For the most part it is stylistically straightforward but it contains two surprising sequences—an amusing dream scene, where the middle-aged heroine imagines herself courted by a dandy, and a flashback to naked soldiers, which introduces a sudden, disrupting element of brutality.

As for contemporary drama, two first features should be mentioned: *Structure of Crystals* (1969) and *Shifting Sands* (1969). *Structure of Crystals* directed by Krzysztof Zanussi, deals with the reunion of two people who were students together.

Malgorzata Braunek in Wladislaw Ślesicki's *Shifting Sands* (1969)

Marek, who has become an extremely successful physicist, has come to visit Jan, who has chosen to work at a remote weather-station. The film deals with their attempt to re-establish a relationship, showing how each questions the ideals, motives and integrity of the other. The plot is treated in a very sober manner. There are no arguments yet the two men can no longer understand each other and there is a hint that the wife is becoming interested in the newcomer. All this is subtly handled, the scientific references are well documented, and the film does touch on problems of professional integrity and the moral obligations of the scientist, yet it all lacks a certain dynamism.

Shifting Sands by Wladyslaw Ślesicki, an established documentary film-maker, is set on the Baltic sea coast which is lovingly filmed and exploited to the full. A father takes his son on holiday and the two become very close until the arrival of a young girl who arouses the father's interest and makes the boy bitterly jealous. Thus the atmosphere of friendship between father and son is completely shattered.

These two films are beautifully made and are far removed from the socialist realist films of the early fifties, but neither of the directors has placed a truly distinctive stamp of originality on his first feature. Beside Wajda's *Landscape after a Battle*, which reworks certain of his and Poland's central obsessions, these new features, and the other films of the end of the sixties, appear very lightweight.

In 1968 film production groups in Poland were reorganized and censorship appeared to become stricter. Certain films became unavailable—for example, *Samson*, in which Wajda had portrayed persecution of the Jews. And *Landscape after a Battle* is reputed to have had censorship troubles. In August 1970 Jerzy Andrzejewski, author of *Ashes and Diamonds*, at the grave of a dead friend, spoke of art in Poland in terms of 'spiritual starvation amid a wilderness of silence'. Whether the Gdansk incidents of December 1970 will lead to liberalization remains to be seen.

Hungary

In the immediate postwar period, Hungary produced one or two interesting features such as Geza Radvanyi's *Somewhere in Europe* (1947). In 1948 the film industry was nationalized but the political climate was already worsening. Béla Balázs, the most important theorist on film aesthetics in Hungary, was dismissed and died shortly after. There ensued the bleak period of socialist realism but towards the mid-fifties a few interesting films began to appear—Károly Makk's *Liliomfi* (1954), Félix Mariássy's *A Glass of Beer* (1955), Zoltán Fábri's *Merry-go-round* (1955). The political upheavals of 1956 disrupted all walks of life but despite initial appearances led to developments which mark Hungary as 'the pacemaker of reform in the Soviet sphere' (*Guardian*, 13 April 1970). The Béla Balázs studio was founded in 1957 and by the early sixties was a lively part of the Hungarian film world; indeed many of the most interesting young directors were able to make shorts with help from its funds. By the late sixties Miklós Jancsó had become established as one of the world's leading directors and in Hungary a whole new 'school' of film-makers had emerged.

Before examining Jancsó's works, however, it is necessary to consider the films of Zoltán Fábri, one of the first postwar directors from Hungary to be praised abroad. *Merry-go-round* (1955) is at first sight a banal love story but it deals with important social themes including the attitude of youth to tradition and the difficulty of adapting to changing circumstances. It is a very lyrical film especially in the scene where the lovers meet on the merry-go-round of the title. *Professor Hannibal* (1956) is the story of a timid teacher who publishes a book on Hannibal. The authorities, much to the teacher's surprise, accuse him of falsifying history. He is unwilling to retract and gradually becomes a hero figure. The film is a strange mixture of styles—satire, fantasy, farce, tragedy—and the ending is ambiguous since the teacher does seem on the point of retracting when he accidently falls to his death. *Professor Hannibal* was first shown in the weeks preceding the events of 1956 and although it is ultimately

Mari Töröcsik, Imre Sós in Zoltán Fábri's *Merry-go-round* (1955)

Ernö Szabó in Fábri's *Professor Hannibal* (1956)

ambiguous, although the setting is the thirties, at the time it seemed very much in tune with the mood of protest.

In these films Fábri showed himself to be interested in social and political problems as well as willing to experiment with style. This is also true of his very mature and complex film, *Twenty Hours* (1964) which deals with postwar history in a small Hungarian village. At the heart of the work is the changing relationship between four men who helped organize the collectivization of the land at the end of the war. The story is told through a complex series of flashbacks and the anchor of the film is a journalist, or perhaps investigator, trying to write a report on events in the village. This is extremely difficult as is illustrated in the striking scene where he is shown sitting on top of a hill brooding on the impossibility of his task—which is visually emphasized by the wind scattering his sheets of paper. Yet the film *Twenty Hours* is itself an attempt to 'write' the report and, like the scattered

Janos Görbe, Antal Páger in Fábri's *Twenty Hours* (1964)

sheets of paper, it is a work which at first sight seems made up of disparate elements. Gradually, however, one pieces together the 'story' of the four men—how they grow apart, how violence flares up, how one of the men shoots another down. In the context of this village Fábri is touching not only on events in Hungary of 1956 but also on a whole range of human, social and philosophical problems. It is, however, a very far cry from the socialist realist approach to contemporary events or that of the Hollywood 'message' film, for it is ultimately open-ended, encouraging debate.

While Fábri was gaining esteem as a feature director in the fifties, Miklós Jancsó was beginning his cinema career in the field of newsreels and shorts. He has described his first feature, *The Bells have gone to Rome* (1958), as naïve, even for the time. His second feature *Cantata* (1963) is a psychological work, very different from his later films, dealing with a doctor who comes to question his friends, his values, his life. It is with Jancsó's next work *My Way Home* (1964) that one first sees real evidence of the cinematic qualities for which he has become famous. In this film, set at the end of the Second World War, a Hungarian taken prisoner by the Russians is placed in the custody of a young soldier who looks after the cattle in the hills. This is, perhaps, the most 'human' of Jancsó's later films since an ill-defined friendship is shown growing up between the two men. For a moment the hostile universe seems to recede but when the young Russian dies the Hungarian is thrown back into a world where men are hunted, humiliated, stripped and beaten. Despite the open spaces, used in this and in most of Jancsó's films, the spectator constantly feels that the characters are hemmed in ; this paradoxical effect is created by such features as the menacing aeroplane which returns from time to time, as if to spy on the characters, or the horse-riders who appear from nowhere to hunt a man down. Yet the approach is not emotional, the actors are encouraged to underplay and the director is very concerned with formal elegance.

Adam Szirtes in Fábri's *Twenty Hours*

András Kozák, Sergei Nikonenko in Miklós Jancsó's *My Way Home* (1964)

Jancsó's *My Way Home*

These features are even more in evidence in Jancsó's next feature, *The Round-up* (1965) for which the director chooses the period after the abortive revolution of 1848 against the Habsburgs. Set in a prison camp amidst the vast plains, the film is concerned with the cruel insidious way by which the captives and perhaps man in general, can be bullied, tricked and humiliated into betrayal. By offering one man his freedom for treachery, by beating to death a woman known to be attached to the revolutionaries, by falsely encouraging hopes of pardon, the captors succeed in their cruel task of weeding out the supporters of the rebel leader Kossuth.

Jancsó's *The Round Up* (1965)

Jancsó's *The Round Up*

Jancsó's *The Red and the White* (1967)

Jancsó's *The Red and the White*

In *The Round-up* the captor/captive, pursuer/pursued relationship is reasonably clear but in *The Red and the White* (1967) it is
much more blurred. Set in Russia in 1918, its chief protagonist
('hero' is too positive a word) is a young Hungarian whose regiment has fought with the Red army. The film opens with a White
cavalryman coldly shooting down a Red soldier and this unfeeling
cruelty is continued throughout the film: herded together by the
Whites the Reds are stripped and told to run for their lives; a
soldier is brutally lanced to death in a river where he is hiding;
wounded prisoners are casually shot through the head. But this
cruelty is inflicted not only by the Whites. The Reds who arrive
at a field hospital where some of their numbers have been hiding,

Jancsó's *The Confrontation* (1969)

mistakenly execute the very nurse who has humiliated herself to save one of the concealed men.

In all these films one is struck by the almost balletic movements and groupings of the actors. In *The Confrontation* (1969) the director pushes this to an extreme by making what could almost be described as a musical. Set in 1947, the film deals with the attempt by young students to create People's Colleges free from the obscurantism of religion. These young reformers constantly burst into song, join hands and dance. Yet despite the superficial gaiety, despite the colour and the change of setting (no longer the vast plains) Jancsó's concern with pursuit, persecution and humiliation is again in evidence. The leader of the reformers does not wish to win over the Catholic students by force but the atmosphere changes with the arrival of a police officer who asks for help in weeding out reactionary elements. When the leader refuses he is dismissed by his group and replaced by a girl whose methods are very different, for she believes in political terrorism. Finally the girl is herself dismissed by her superiors but the film ends on a disturbing note. The police chief tells the girl not to worry since one day she will certainly find herself again in a position of power, which would seem to imply that repression inevitably returns. Understandably, *The Confrontation* ran into trouble with the authorities, but to see this so-called 'parable' only as a satire of the socialist system is to limit its range of reference. In this and in all his films Jancsó is concerned, as he himself said, with the 'question of power and repression' in general, with 'man's relation to power and repression'. The work of Miklós Jancsó presents a fairly bleak vision of the world since, at all the different periods of history evoked, the individual is shown to be corrupted, humiliated and destroyed by those who exercise power.

For certain critics, however, these films are too cold, too formal. It is true that Jancsó avoids sentimentality, that his actors, especially András Kozák who appears in almost all his films, are encouraged to play down their emotions. This is deliberate on the director's part for he has admitted that he is capable of being violently partisan. Like Flaubert, Jancsó has tried to abstract himself emotionally from his works and to infuse his style with the 'greatest dryness and simplicity possible'; and like Brecht, whom Jancsó does not admire but to whom he has been compared, he would seem to want the spectator to meditate on his works without becoming too emotionally involved. In certain of his films, including *My Way Home* and *The Red and the White,* by ending with a close-up of the questioning, bewildered face of András Kozák, he appears to make a direct invitation to the audience to meditate on what they have seen.

The films of Miklós Jancsó are instantly recognizable; he deliberately avoids psychology and concentrates on form; if the camera is not restlessly prowling in lateral tracking-shots, the characters on the screen are constantly in movement; shots are often composed for an aesthetic rather than a dramatic effect. And in all his works there are recurrent images which take on a deep significance—the aeroplane, the horses, the men stripped naked and hunted. While these films appeal aesthetically and the problems they present are of universal significance, Miklós Jancsó is very much a product of a country which has known centuries of violent changes of power.

Jancsó's *The Confrontation*

Zoltán Latinovits, Tibor Szilágyi in András Kovác's *Cold Days* (1966)

András Kovács, a contemporary and friend of Jancsó, is concerned with dilemmas of conscience, with individual and collective responsibility, with social injustices. His courageous short,
Difficult People (1964) showed how many Hungarian artists
and designers remain ignored at home while their work is admired
abroad. The film which gained him international renown was his
feature *Cold Days* (1966), based on a novel about the massacre of
over three thousand people carried out by Hungarian troops in
northern Czechoslovakia during the war. The victims were shot,
then their bodies pushed through holes in the iced-over river. In
a prison, some years after the incident, four soldiers of different
rank are awaiting trial. As they talk and argue, trying to shift
responsibility, the days of the massacre are evoked in flashback.
The wife and son of the highest-ranking officer went missing
during these 'cold days' but he insists that they must be still
alive. The film shows how they became innocent victims. It is

perhaps this personal element which brings home the nature of the appalling massacre. Unlike Jancsó, Kovács does not show the cruel slaughter. The preparations on the ice are shown, shots are heard, but that is all. Like all the 'new' Hungarian films, *Cold Days* invites discussion. The four men are not presented as black

András Kovác's *Cold Days*

villains—the film shows how they came to be involved and various turning points when they could have chosen to act differently. The questions raised concern conscience and responsibility. *Cold Days* is a sober, controlled film, full of restrained irony.

Tamás Rényi is slightly younger than Jancsó and Kovács but is of their generation. His first features tended to deal with postwar Hungary and the problems facing the working classes. His fifth feature *Deadlock* (1966) has been distributed in the West and does have fine visual qualities but ultimately it is not much more than a love story which ends in murder. A more interesting work is his next feature, *The Valley* (1967). Set in the past, during a war, it shows how a group of deserters take refuge in a village in the valley of the title. There are only women and children here, since the men are absent fighting. The arrival of the deserters puts a strain on this community and most of the film is concerned with the portrayal of the tensions and jealousy between the frustrated women. The war, however, breaks into the valley when the enemy soldiers arrive and slay everyone—ironically on the very day that peace is declared. The film ends with the returning husbands and sons vainly searching the village for signs of life. The pathos of the scene is heightened by the use of a high-angle long-shot showing the men running into the various houses and by their expectant cries of greeting which punctuate the sound track. There are

Tamás Rényi's *Deadlock* (1966)

Rényi's *The Valley* (1967)

echoes of Jancsó in this film: the same casual approach to violence, as in the scene where victims are seen tied on to the turning sails of a windmill; the same restrained acting, especially that of the leading man played by Gábor Koncz; the same concern for composition in the grouping of the protagonists. Yet the story line is perhaps too strongly developed for the film to succeed as a comment on life in general, as would appear to be the intention, and the menacing hints that the women are going to turn on the men are never realized.

The films of most of the younger Hungarian directors have been

Ivan Andonov, Gyorgy Banffy in István Gaál's *The Falcons* (1970)

little seen in the West. One reads of the new features of Sándor
Sára, Pál Gábor, Judit Elek and so on, but, despite their success at
festivals throughout the world, few Hungarian films find distributors in Britain or the US. One is therefore obliged to concentrate on films which have been reasonably widely shown, those of
directors István Gaál, Ferenc Kósa and István Szabó.

István Gaál's fourth feature, *The Falcons* (1970), has been
praised as his best film and gained the special jury prize at Cannes.
Shot in Eastman colour, it is set on the Hungarian plains and
shows the arrival of a young man at a centre where, for scientific

Ferenc Kósa's *Ten Thousand Suns* (1967)

reasons, falcons are trained to hunt. The filming of the birds is extraordinary, the fruit perhaps of Gaál's experience in the documentary field. This is not, however, simply a nature film, it has a deeper significance. The authoritarian rule of the chief trainer, his fanaticism, his reference to the falcons as the 'police of the air' all point to a comment on totalitarianism. At the end of the film, the young man runs away from this society where he feels his liberty being eaten away. All this is very subtly handled and the director avoids emotionalism.

Ferenc Kósa's *Ten Thousand Suns* (1967) was planned as the

first feature of the Béla Balázs studio. It is an attempt to reflect recent Hungarian history by tracing thirty years in the life of a peasant family. It raises a whole series of issues—collectivization of the land, the events of 1956, the difficulty of adapting to change, individual liberty and social responsibility. The film is beautifully made, but the French critic Michel Delahaye has accused it of presenting a falsified picture. He points out that the authorities made changes to the script and says that the result is something akin to a screenplay on the events in France of May 1968, rewritten by President Pompidou !

The most appealing of the younger directors whose work has reached the West is István Szabó. He does not avoid the social, moral and political problems that concern the other directors but his films are far more lyrical and intimate. Szabó's first feature, *The Age of Daydreaming* (1964) concerns the political and sentimental development of a group of young people. The hero, beautifully acted by András Bálint, is a young television engineer who falls in love with a girl he sees in the studio. When the two finally meet (after he has had an unfortunate affair elsewhere) their relationship is disappointingly fruitless. While tracing this story the film touches on many issues, especially the problems of youthful idealism and the realities of society. *Father* (1966) is a delightful film which deserves to be more widely known. The father of the title dies at the end of the war when his son is very young. The film traces the growth to manhood of this boy. He has only three real memories of his father but he creates fantasies about him, uses these to impress his friends and comes to believe them himself. While a young student the hero still lives on the imagined exploits of his father and he wears his watch and leather coat but at last he decides to try to find out the truth. The final sequence in the cemetery would seem to signify that the young man has at last truly accepted that his father is dead, that he will now try to live his own life. There is much in the film that recalls the techniques of the French New Wave—the humorous fantasy sequences with the father as a bold partisan, a politician, a distinguished surgeon—and like Truffaut whom he admires Szabó shows great understanding of childhood and youth. Yet

András Bálint in István Szabó's *Age of Daydreaming* (1964)

this is very much a Hungarian film, set against the background of the postwar years, and the work of an extremely talented director.

Szabó stands out from his fellow 'new' directors by his lyricism —although politics and social questions are not absent from his films. In the other directors such concerns are treated in a much more sober, intellectual manner. These films, which exist side by side with a much more 'popular' cinema in Hungary in the shape of musicals, rustic comedies and so on, do not offer simple, socialist realist solutions but attempt to encourage discussion on complex social and political problems.

on pages 88–9
Miriam Kantorková, Jaromír Hanzlík in Otakar Vávra's *Romance for Trumpet* (1966)

Miklós Gábor in István Szabó's *Father* (1966)

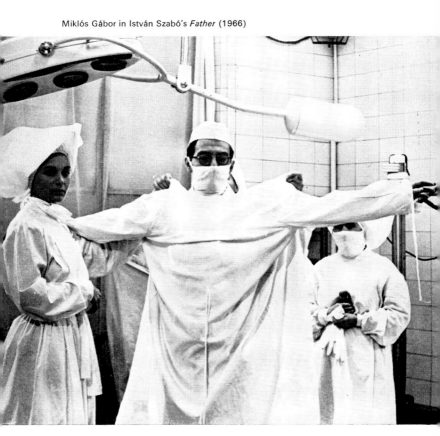

Jana Brejchová, Gustav Valach in Karel Kachyňa's *The Night of the Bride* (1967)

Czechoslovakia

Czechoslovakia has a long cinematic history and by the early thirties Prague had the most modern studios in Europe. In 1932 the film *Ecstasy* by Gustav Machatý caused a scandal throughout the world with its famous nude scene and made a star of its actress, Heddy Kiesler (Hedy Lamarr). At the same time, the thirties saw the debuts of Martin Frič and Otakar Vávra, who continued to make films right into the sixties.

Despite this tradition, the nationalized Czechoslovak cinema was very disappointing in the immediate postwar years, except in the field of animation. In the late fifties films began to become more adventurous but the growing liberalization was halted in 1959. Certain features were attacked and banned, and film-makers were told to concentrate on the portrayal of more 'positive' heroes. By the time these banned films were released in 1963 the political climate was changing and the Czechoslovak cinema was entering the period of extraordinary creative activity that was to last, despite sporadic attempts to tighten the screw, until 1968.

These years saw the emergence of a group of exciting young directors but many older, established film-makers produced works that merit attention. The veteran Otakar Vávra, who as a lecturer at FAMU, the Prague film school, taught many of the leading figures in the Czech New Wave, continues to make features that can stand comparison with those of his distinguished pupils. *Romance for Trumpet* (1966) is an extremely poetic work based on a ballad by František Hrubín. Constructed around a man's nostalgic memories of his first idyllic romance, Vávra's film is distinguished by its feeling for nature and its counterpoint of love and death, idealism and earthy sensuality.

Karel Kachyňa who was one of the first graduates from the Prague film school, began directing in the fifties, at first in partnership with his contemporary Vojtěch Jasný. In *The Night of the Bride* (1967) Kachyňa turns to the sort of socio-political issue that is the concern of many of the modern Hungarian film-makers. More lyrical, more intimate, more amusing than its Hungarian counterparts, this film is set in a small Moravian village and deals with the problems involved in collectivism. The dramatic tension in *Night of the Bride* is created by the return from a convent of a novice who leads the villagers in revolt on Christmas Eve. This character, with her underlying sensuality, her masochistic delight in walking barefoot through the snow, her puritanical treatment of her idiot servant that borders on sadism, is portrayed by Jana Brejchová, the leading young Czech actress. Her chief opponent, the tiny communist official of the village, well acted by Minislav Hofman, is for much of the film a figure of fun, but he does ultimately appear as courageous and sympathetic. Nevertheless *Night of the Bride* does not follow a strict doctrinaire line and is very different from a socialist realist work; at the same time it shows great concern for formal beauty: the composition of the shots, the figures standing out against the snowy landscape, the use of the wide screen all make Kachyňa's film a visual delight.

Of all the older directors, however, the most famous and most influential are Ján Kadár and Elmar Klos who began working as a team in 1952. After the banning of *The Three Wishes* in 1959, Kadár and Klos did not make another feature until *Death is Called Engelchen* which appeared in 1963. Their most famous film *The Shop on the High Street* appeared in 1965. The setting is a small Czech town during the Second World War. Tono, a carpenter, dislikes his brother-in-law, the fascist leader of the community, but for personal rather than ideological reasons; when the latter asks Tono to requisition a shop on the high street, the carpenter is pressed by his wife to accept. The shop is run by a deaf old Jewish woman on whom Tono takes pity and he gradually finds that he is being forced into taking sides. By helping her he is opposing the fascist regime. When the Hinka guards begin to round up the Jews to transport them to concentration camps, Tono is faced with a moral crisis: should he save her at the risk of his own life? The old woman is incapable of understanding what is happening and in exasperation the carpenter pushes her roughly and accidentally kills her. In despair he commits suicide. Tono's growing awareness, his feelings of guilt, his moments of coward-ice, all raise the question of the responsibility of the individual to fight prejudice and oppression. *The Shop on the High Street* is not, however, a gloomy tragedy: it begins in an atmosphere of near farce but as the film progresses, the humour slips away and the relationship develops between the carpenter and the old woman, beautifully portrayed by J. Kroner and the Polish actress Ida Kaminska. The film ends with an imaginative dream-sequence, in high key and slow motion, showing Tono floating along in the sunshine with the old woman on his arm.

J. Kroner, Ida Kaminska in *The Shop on the High Street* (1965) by Ján Kadár and Elmar Klos

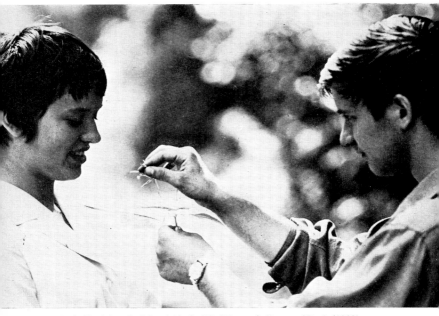

Paula Martinkov, Ladislav Jakim in Miloš Forman's *Peter and Pavla* (1963)

Concern with serious moral and social problems, the blending of humour and tragedy, the willingness to exploit stylistic techniques that create a certain element of fantasy, these features in the films of Kadár and Klos reflect the qualities of the whole New Wave of young Czechoslovak directors of the mid-sixties.

One of the first of these to make his mark was Miloš Forman whose feature *Peter and Pavla* appeared in 1963. Forman specializes in the portrayal of everyday life, of ordinary individuals who are neither 'positive' heroes nor tortured anti-heroes. Peter, the main male character in the director's first work, is an unexciting

Vladimir Pucholt in Forman's *Peter and Pavla*

young man who has started his first job as a store detective. The film shows his clumsiness at work and his relationships with the girl Pavla, who is not really interested in him, and with his parents, especially his pompous, convention-bound father. What is important in this touching, humorous work is not the story but rather the fine observation of human behaviour and the remarkably convincing performances that Forman draws from his actors, Paula Martinkov and Ladislav Jakim in the title rôles, and especially Vladimir Pucholt as a nervous young worker who borrows money from Peter.

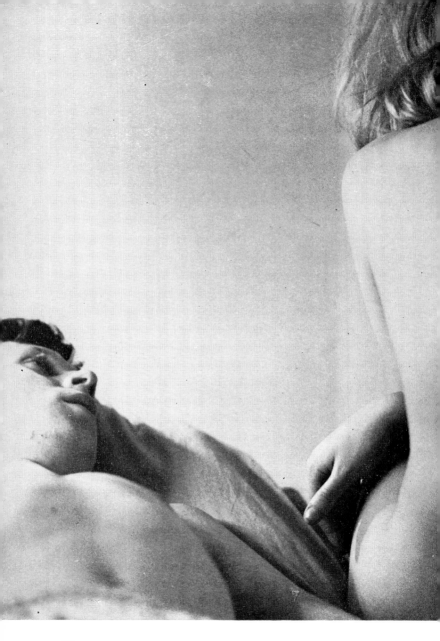

Pucholt is the leading male actor in Forman's next film, *A Blonde in Love* (1965). A young factory worker, acted by the talented Jana Brejchová, falls in love with a pianist in a dance band. For her the meeting is an intense emotional experience. For him it is merely the affair of one night. The girl goes to visit the boy in his home town, which embarrasses him and shocks his parents. In this amusing sequence the director pokes fun at the narrow-minded older generation, while arousing compassion for the girl. Throughout the film the director casts an ironic eye on contemporary Czech society and on human foibles in general. In both these films Forman uses a dance-hall sequence to observe man the social animal. He shows the girls trying to attract attention while pretending to remain aloof, the boys drinking to obtain Dutch courage, the soldiers, in *A Blonde in Love*, removing their wedding rings in the hope of finding a woman for the night.

A dance-hall is the setting of Forman's third feature, *The Firemen's Ball* (1967), which shows how a social function goes haywire. The firemen's celebrations are interrupted when they are called out on duty. On their return, they find that all the tombola prizes have been stolen. The crowning disaster occurs when the old commander of the force is given a presentation for his services —the box, which should have contained a gilt axe, is empty, this too has been stolen. In all his films Forman shows sympathy for

Vladimir Pucholt and Jana Brejchová in Forman's *A Blonde in Love* (1965)

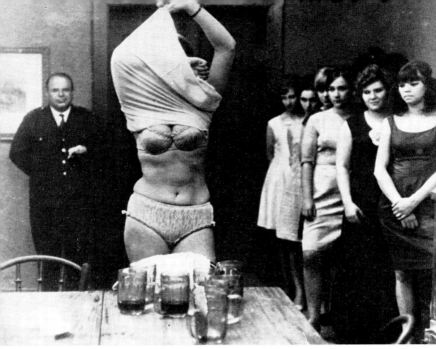

Forman's *The Firemen's Ball* (1967)

the disappointments of his characters but in *The Firemen's Ball,*
which concentrates on the older generation, poking fun at
convention and tradition, he infuses his humour with a more
biting note of satire.

Ivan Passer, who wrote the scripts of these three films, directed
Intimate Lighting (1965) which is in the same territory as the films
of Forman. A musician from the town, accompanied by his playful
mistress, visits an old friend who lives in the country with his wife,
children and parents. After spending a day and night, during which
the friends talk, attend a funeral and play music together, the
visitors prepare to leave. Thus the film has virtually no plot and no
drama, in the conventional sense of the word, but Passer, like

Jan Vostrčil in Ivan Passer's *Intimate Lighting* (1965)

Forman, records telling little actions which reveal the underlying
tensions and disappointments in the characters. This is very much
in evidence in the meal scene where the members of the host's
family argue over the sharing out of the parts of the chicken. The
film suggests the disillusionment of the married man, who,
unlike his friend, has sacrificed his liberty for material comforts—
his house, his car. As in *Peter and Pavla*, the film ends with a
sudden freeze of the action, the implication being that this is a
reflection of 'real' life which does not offer satisfying conclusions.
The wry humour tinged with compassion that one finds in the
films of Miloš Forman is not, however, so evident in *Intimate
Lighting*.

Jiří Menzel's *Balthazar's Death* in *Pearls of the Deep* (1965)

In 1965 *Pearls of the Deep* appeared, an anthology film based on the short stories of the leading Czech author Bohumil Hrabal. Ivan Passer was to contribute an episode but his short, *A Boring Afternoon*, was released separately since it was felt that otherwise the film would be too long. As it stands *Pearls of the Deep* contains episodes of five of Czechoslovakia's leading young directors: Jiří Menzel, Evald Schorm, Jan Němec, Věra Chytilová, Jaromil Jireš.

Jiří Menzel's episode *Balthazar's Death*, a strange little film tinged with fantasy, describes a family's visit to a motor cycle rally. Nothing of the racing is shown, only the reaction of the spectators and especially those of the family, who, when the favourite is killed, declare how lucky they are to be present at yet another fatal accident. *Closely Observed Trains* (1966) which shot Menzel to international fame and won an Oscar in 1968, is also based on a work by Bohumil Hrabal. It is set during the Second World War. The young, inexperienced hero reminds one somewhat

of the young man in *Peter and Pavla* but much more happens than
in any of the works of Miloš Forman : there is the developing story
of the main protagonist with his attempted suicide, his first taste
of sex, his death ; there is also an amusing sub-plot concerning
the sex-obsessed assistant station-master and containing the
memorably funny sequence where he rubber-stamps a girl's

Václav Neckar in Jiří Menzel's *Closely Observed Trains* (1966)

Rudolf Hrušinský, František Rehák, Vlastimil Brodský in Jiří Menzel's
Capricious Summer (1968)

bottom. The humour of the film is, however, tinged with a black
comedy evident in the scene where the hero tries to cut his wrists—
and in the almost casual way that he is killed, trying to sabotage a
train.

Menzel's next feature, *Capricious Summer* (1968), adapted by
the director from a humorous Czech novel, is beautifully shot in
colour and is very different in mood from his first feature. The plot
concerns three middle-aged friends, a priest, a major and a
bathing-pool attendant, who meet, drink and argue in a lively but
friendly way. This routine is disturbed by the arrival of an acrobat
and his charming assistant, Anna. The three men in turn flirt with
the girl but each is humiliated. The wife of the bathing-pool
attendant moves in with the acrobat, the priest almost loses an ear
in a struggle with some shocked villagers, the major is beaten
with a stick. When the acrobat and his assistant finally leave, the
three friends and the wife fall back into the routine of their lives.

on pages 104–5
Jan Kačer in Evald Schorm's *Return of the Prodigal Son* (1966)

The relationships between the three men are delicately portrayed and the film has great whimsical charm. At the same time there is a black side to the comedy, which links *Capricious Summer* to *Balthazar's Death* and *Closely Observed Trains*: this can be seen in the rather sadistic close-up of the priest's ear being sown up with a fish-hook by the bathing-pool attendant.

The acrobat in *Capricious Summer* is portrayed by Menzel himself who enjoys acting and has played rôles in many films

Jiří Menzel in his *Capricious Summer*

Schorm's *House of Joy* in *Pearls of the Deep* (1965)

including those of Evald Schorm, the 'conscience' of the New Wave in Czechoslovakia. Schorm's first feature *Courage for Every Day* (1964) immediately ran into trouble with the authorities who held up its release for many months. The hero, Jarda, refuses to admit that his political ideals have been wrong and, as a result, loses his mistress and friends. Jarda's gradual disillusionment and final recognition of the truth can be seen as an illustration of 'de-Stalinization' on an individual level. Schorm's next film was the bizarre episode in *Pearls of the Deep* entitled *The House of Joy*. Filmed in garish colour, this short work showed the visit of two insurance agents to the house of a primitive painter. To interpret the main rôle Schorm used a genuine primitive painter, Václav

Jana Brejchová, Jan Kačer in Schorm's *Return of the Prodigal Son*

Zak, said to have inspired Hrubal's story in the first place. The film shows the inability of conventional social structures, represented by the insurance agents, to cope with the original individual, represented by the artist.

The problem of individual liberty and the pressures of convention is a major theme in Schorm's most impressive feature, *The Return of the Prodigal Son* (1966). The hero, Jan, is being treated in a mental hospital after an unsuccessful attempt to commit suicide. His wife, his colleagues, his psychiatrist find him bewildering, for he was 'happily' married and 'well established' in his work. Despite his desire to leave the asylum, Jan suffers great anguish on the occasions when he is allowed to return to everyday life. His problem is that he is unwilling to compromise his conscience in order to fit into the accepted social structures. At the same time he can detect the repressed despair in the very people who find him bewildering. Jan is an outsider and the society in which he lives alienates and persecutes anyone who will not conform—this would appear to be the sense of the sequence towards the end of the film where he is mistakenly hunted as an assassin by a mob of peasants. *The Return of the Prodigal Son*, beautifully acted by Jan Kačer and Jana Brejchová, is a challenging and moving film which evokes the despair of the individual who is at odds with society. It is not astonishing that the authorities placed a virtual ban on this film when it was first released.

By contrast, *Pastor's End* (1968) is a declared farce with echoes of Fernandel's Don Camillo series. Schorm's serious intent is, however, not absent from this tale of a sexton who poses as a village priest, thereby engaging in a power struggle with the socialist teacher. The film is an earthy, comic yet finally moving reworking of the life of Christ and Schorm shows individual initiative hampered by rigid institutionalism, here symbolized by the church. And the comic secret police in the film gradually take on a more sinister significance : in the last image after the death of the sexton, the three village police, supported by many others, are shown closing in on the village—a disturbing conclusion, especially in the light of the events of 1968.

Evald Schorm is deeply concerned with the problems of personal idealism and social repression. His works seem to have become increasingly pessimistic yet contain a plea, a despairing one perhaps, for tolerance and liberty.

Jan Němec is a director who seems to share this pessimism and concern with the outsider. His approach, however, is much less sober than that of Schorm. Němec's first feature, *Diamonds of the Night* (1964), shows two prisoners of war escaping from a train in the Second World War. As Němec shows them running through the countryside, he interposes, without warning, the memories, dreams and associations running through the mind of one of the fugitives. Bursting into a farm in search of food the young man is faced by the woman of the house. His violent thoughts, of rape

Ladislav Jánsky Antonín Kumbera in Jan Němec's *Diamonds of the Night* (1964)

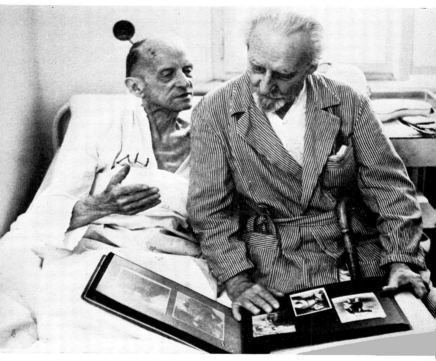

Milos Ctrnacty, Frantisek Havel in Němec's *The Impostors* in *Pearls of the Deep* (1965)

◀ Ilse Bischofá in Němec's *Diamonds of the Night*

and murder, are visually translated. Thus the over-all effect of the film is dreamlike or even nightmarish, especially in the depiction of the grotesque old men who hunt down the fleeing prisoners.

The Impostors (1965), Němec's contribution to *Pearls of the Deep,* could also be described as grotesque. Two old men tell each other of the exploits of their past, but after they die it is shown that both were inveterate liars.

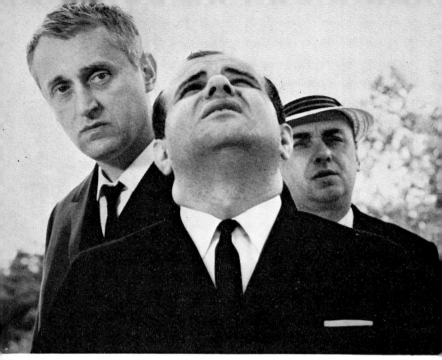

Evald Schorm, Karel Mareš, Pavel Bošek in Němec's *The Party and the Guests* (1966)

Němec's *The Party and the Guests* ▶

Both these films have a disturbing quality which is even more in evidence in Němec's famous *The Party and the Guests* (1966). In this sinister fable a group of friends are seen making their way to a country party when they are suddenly surrounded by a gang of threatening men. The friends are forced to play a game that becomes increasingly more frightening until, at last, the host appears and leads them to the party. One of the new arrivals steals away but the film ends with the host sending out dogs and armed men to hunt him down.

This fascinating film, with its echoes of Kafka and its surrealist scenes such as the banquet beside the lake, would seem to be, on the one hand, an attack on totalitarian rule; on the other, a satire of those who, by conforming, condone persecution and atrocity. (It is interesting that the guest who, refusing to compromise, leaves the party is played by Evald Schorm.) Němec himself

Marta Kubisova, Petr Kopriva in Němec's *Martyrs of Love* (1966):
The Temptations of a White-Collar Worker

Hana Kuberova in Němec's *Martyrs of Love: Nastenka's Reveries* ▶

talked of this film, which was banned by the authorities for almost
two years, in the following terms:

How pleasant it is to take part in all the parties life offers. To sit
down at a well-laid table and leave behind the cares and worries
you cannot do anything about in any case; to live, and above all,
to survive, that is the credo of people and societies. . . .

Němec's third feature, *Martyrs of Love* (also 1966), is made up of
three episodes about timid people who long for romance. The
first sequence, *The Temptations of a White-Collar Worker*, shows
the unsuccessful attempt by a shy civil servant to realize his dream
of seducing a girl. In *Nastenka's Reveries* a waitress imagines a
love affair with a handsome officer and a debonair singer. The

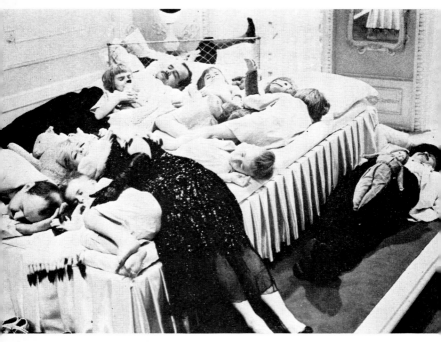

Němec's *Martyrs of Love: Orphan Rudolph's Adventure*

third episode, *Orphan Rudolph's Adventure*, shows how a car mechanic penetrates into a stately house where a beautiful woman shows interest in him and asks him to return later, but unfortunately Rudolph cannot find the house again. The film ends with the three 'martyrs of love' meeting at a crossroads and walking off side by side. Němec presents these three 'gloomy farces', as he calls them, in a highly imaginative manner, drawing on memories of silent films but creating an atmosphere of disturbing fantasy that is entirely his own.

Jaromil Jireš and Věra Chytilová have both used fantasy in

Jaromil Jireš's *The Cry* (1963)

their films. Jireš's first feature, *The Cry* (1963), takes, however, a
contemporary setting. While a young television repairman goes
his rounds, his wife is in labour in hospital. The film is stylistically
quite inventive, introducing, without warning, the man's memories
of different periods in his relationship with his wife and cutting
backwards and forwards between the husband at work and the
wife in hospital. This allows the director to deal with the problems
of marriage while at the same time he presents a varied picture of
contemporary Czechoslovakian society through the different
premises visited by the television engineer.

117

Dana Valtova in Jireš's *Romance* in *Pearls of the Deep* (1965)

Romance, Jireš's contribution to *Pearls of the Deep*, is an unremarkable little film distinguished only by the warmth and sensuality of the actress playing the gypsy girl. His second feature, *The Joke* (1968), takes an ironic look at the rigidly conformist atmosphere of the fifties. With his third feature, *Valerie and her Week of Wonders* (1969), Jireš enters the realm

Jaromil Jireš's *Valerie and her Week of Wonders* (1969)

of fantasy. Based on a famous Czech surrealist novel of the
interwar period, the film interweaves imaginary adventures of
a young girl with the real events of a week in her life. Shot in
beautiful colour, *Valerie and her Week of Wonders* is an extremely
poetic film which juxtaposes visions of beauty with images of
horror.

Věra Chytilová's *The World of Self-Service* in *Pearls of the Deep* (1965)

Věra Chytilová's episode in *Pearls of the Deep*, entitled *The World of Self-Service*, starts off in an atmosphere of everyday reality that recalls Miloš Forman. When a bride and a young man who has been searching for his girl-friend go off into the night the mood changes and the film ends in an atmosphere of fantasy. Chytilová's most famous film is the bizarre comedy *Daisies* (1966), imaginatively shot in colour by the director's husband Jaroslav Kučera and it relies almost entirely on visual effects. The film traces the actions of two girls who are totally selfish and completely irresponsible. Chytilová has said that her original intention was to show the false values by which man lives but that the completed film is about 'destruction or the desire to destroy'. Unfortunately the film is far too strained and the attempt to give it wider implications by the juxtaposition of war images at the beginning and by the atomic explosion at the end is clumsy and unoriginal.

Jitka Cerhova, Ivana Karbanova in Chytilová's *Daisies* (1966)

Pavel Juráček, one of the collaborators on an early script for *Daisies,* is himself a director. In 1963, together with Jan Schmidt, he made the short feature *Josef Kilián*, which won prizes at many festivals. With its hero's vain search for Josef Kilián and for the shop from where he hired a cat, with its portrayal of people passively accepting bureaucracy, this film is very much a reflection

Josef Kilián (1964) directed by Pavel Juráček and Jan Schmidt

of the world of Franz Kafka. The first feature Juráček directed on
his own was *Every Young Man* (1965), a film in two episodes,
about military service. The first part deals with the relationship
between a corporal and a private, forced to spend the day together.
The corporal begins by haughtily ignoring his inferior in rank,
but by the end of the day, has come to respect the younger man.

Ivan Vyskocil, Pavel Landovsky in Pavel Juráček's *Every Young Man* (1965)

The second episode is much more panoramic, giving a whole series of touching or comic incidents involving all or some of the members of the regiment. *Every Young Man* is a humorous film with satirical touches which shows compassion for the individuals within the regimented atmosphere of military service.

Němec, Chytilová and Juráček create films that have been variously described as fables, allegories or parables in which the logical or chronological order of events is often disrupted. A director who uses similar techniques is Antonin Máša, who wrote the script of Schorm's *Courage for Every Day*. In *Hotel for Strangers*, subtitled 'a mummery about love and death', Máša uses speeded-up action, symbolism and fantasy. In this reconstruction of the diary of a murdered man Máša, like Schorm, shows that the individual who does not conform is destroyed by the world.

This fascinating period of the mid-sixties in the Czechoslovak cinema also produced a number of delightful comedies. *Never Strike a Woman—even with a Flower* (1966), directed by Zdeněk Podskalský, is the amusing story of a middle-aged musician who, despite appearances, is irresistible to women. The film is distinguished by fine performances from Vlastimil Brodský and the ever-present Jana Brejchová, who are in real life husband and wife. *Private Hurricane* (1967), by Hynek Bočan who worked as assistant to Němec and Kachyňa, traces the complex interrelations between three separate couples. The film has moments of black humour when the factory worker, beautifully acted by Pavel Landovsky, makes a series of violent but unsuccessful attempts to kill his boss who is having an affair with his girl-friend. This is a sophisticated film which takes a cynical look at relations between the sexes and the director handles the complex plot structures skilfully. These witty films seem, however, very lightweight in comparison with the more serious, more experimental, more socially critical films of the Czechoslovak New Wave.

Antonín Máša's *Hotel for Strangers* (1966)

126

Jana Brejchová in Zdeněk Podskalský's *Never Strike a Woman—Even with a Flower* (1966)

Josef Somr, Pavel Landovsky in Hynek Bočan's *Private Hurricane* (1967)

Since 1968 only a few new films from Czechoslovakia have been shown abroad. Among these are *Valerie and her Week of Wonders,* already discussed, and *The Deserter and the Nomads* (1968) by the Slovak director Juraj Jukubisko. The film is made up of three episodes, each set at a different period of history, but linked by a recurrent character who is, in fact, Death. Full of images of extreme cruelty, *The Deserter and the Nomads* is a pessimistic allegory of the human condition.

The Cremator (1968) is a first feature by another Slovak director, Juraj Herz. His film is a black comedy set in the late thirties and early war years. Fearful of the consequences of having a Jewish wife, an employee in a crematorium murders first her, then their son. He finally becomes director of the crematorium and is shown to be delighted at the thought of the thousands of 'clients' which fascism will bring him. What is so striking in this horror comedy, is the contrast between the man's middle-class ambitions and the bestial lengths to which he will go to realize them.

Although these three features have been exported, more films were banned in Czechoslovakia in 1969–70 than in all the preceding years since the war—including features by Schorm and Menzel. Many leading directors left the country to work abroad, some may never return. Thus, the New Wave in Czechoslovakia seems to have come to an end in 1968 with the intervention of the Warsaw Pact troops and the resultant political changes.

Juraj Herz's *The Cremator* (1968)

Yugoslavia

The Yugoslav State Film Enterprise was set up in 1945 and studios were established throughout the country. The first films dealt almost exclusively with the Second World War and partisan fighting. War themes, treated in a very conventional manner, continued to dominate the Yugoslav cinema until the sixties when the number of feature films increased and their quality improved beyond recognition. By the late sixties Yugoslavia had produced four or five directors acclaimed abroad.

One of the first to make his mark was Aleksandar Petrović whose feature, *Where Love Has Gone* (1961) is considered as representing the beginning of the Yugoslavian New Wave. The two films for which he is best known abroad are, however, *Tri* (1965) and *I Even Met Some Happy Gypsies* (1967). The former consists of three stories covering various periods of the war but linked by one recurrent character. In the first of these he is more or less an observer, in the second he moves into the foreground as he and a fellow soldier are hunted by a German patrol, in the third, set at the end of the war, he becomes an observer again. Although this film takes place in the Second World War, although the cruelty of the Germans is shown in the second episode, *Tri* is not the conventional war film with good and bad clearly defined. The violence inflicted by the Yugoslav soldiers on an innocent man (in the first episode) and the hero's questioning of the execution of collaborators (in the third episode), show that the director is concerned with wider issues than partisan heroism. He would seem to be illustrating the inevitable cruelties and brutalities inflicted by *all* sides in the context of war. Visually the film is dazzling, especially in the second episode with the use of the telephoto lens, the hand-held camera and the aerial shots that pick out the fugitives hiding in the marshland.

Petrović's next film, shot in colour, is even more stylistically arresting. This is the famous *I Even Met Some Happy Gypsies* (starring the Yugoslav Belmondo, Bekim Fehmiu), which opened simultaneously in four Parisian cinemas. The film follows the

Bata Živojinović in Aleksandar Petrović's *Tri* (1965)

fortunes of a gypsy who trades in goose feathers. His rivalry with another gypsy, complicated by the presence of a girl, ends in murder. What is so striking about this film is its visual brilliance, its rapid pace, its avoidance of conventional storytelling devices (the spectator has to deduce much of what is going on) and its striking portrayal of the gypsy community which is totally at odds with the rest of society. This is shown in the conclusion where none of the gypsies, despite their links with the murdered man, will give the police any help in tracing his assassin. According to the director *I Even Met Some Happy Gypsies* raises the 'problems attached to freedom in a completely uncompromised environment'. Petrović is a director concerned with serious moral and social issues which he portrays in a dazzling style. Indeed he could perhaps be criticized for a rather self-indulgent technical virtuosity.

Bekim Fehmiu in Petrović's *I Even Met Some Happy Gypsies* (1967)

Petrović's *I Even Met Some Happy Gypsies*

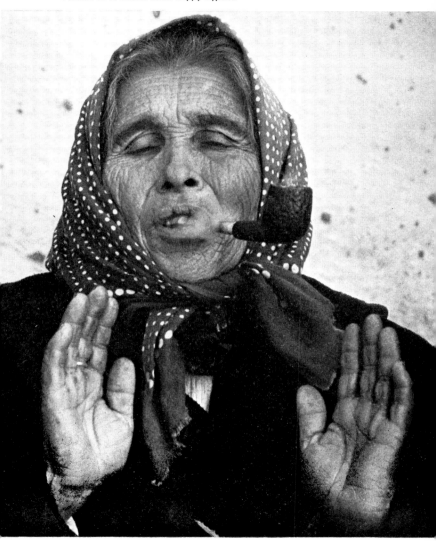

Dragan Nikolić in Živojin Pavlović's *When I'm Dead and White* (1968)

Despite this ebullient style, the muddy gypsy encampment, the bleak slum quarter of the city, even the hero of the *Happy Gypsies*, are features that can be compared to the much starker world of Živojin Pavlović. The people in the films of this more sober director are all doomed to failure. The criminal in *The Return* (1966) tries unsuccessfully to reintegrate himself into society. In *When I'm Dead and White* (1968) Pavlović takes as his hero a drifter, Janko, who lives only for the present. He is ready to lie and cheat to gain his ends, and other human beings, especially women, exist only as long as they satisfy his needs. The people in Pavlović's films, said Peter Cowie (*International Film Guide,* 1969), are 'human refuse, like the prisoners in Dostoievsky's *House of the Dead,* and *When I'm Dead and White* suggests

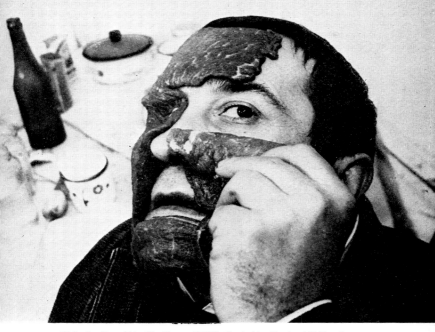

Slobodan Perović in *The Crows* (1969) directed by Gordan Mihić and
Ljubiša Kozomara

that only their urgent life force keeps them afloat in a mean and
vicious society'.

Similar characters are to be found in a first feature, *The Crows*
(1969), made by Gordan Mihić and Ljubiša Kozomara, two
former scriptwriters who have worked with Pavlović. This film is a
strange mixture of violence and humour. The hero, an ex-boxer
and petty thief, cannot fit into society. He is joined by his mad
mother and a strange trio of dancers, two women and a man. As
they bungle attempt after attempt to steal money, the characters
disappear one by one—the mother dies, the three dancers are
killed in turn. The film ends with the ex-boxer returning to his
mother's house but the last shots show the return of the 'dead'
trio, laughing and beckoning. A puzzling ending to a bizarre film.

Milena Dravić, Relja Bašić, Stevo Zigon in *Rondo* (1966) directed by
Žvonimir Berković

Very different from this film and those of Pavlović is the first
feature of Žvonimir Berković entitled *Rondo* (1966). The setting
is for the most part indoors, the action is limited to a game of
chess and to the subtle developments of the relationships between
an artist, his wife and his friend. Every Sunday the friend comes to
the artist's flat to play chess and gradually falls into an affair with
the wife. The chess board is at the centre of the film, the moves
paralleling the emotional developments of the characters. The
title of the film denotes the director's interest in music : 'I remain a
frustrated musician entirely obsessed by the desire to use the film

Janez Uhrovec, Milena Dravić in *Man is not a Bird* (1966) directed by
Dušan Makavejev

medium . . . to obtain the perfection of musical compositional
forms.'

Of all the 'new' Yugoslav directors, the most original is, perhaps,
Dušan Makavejev. His first feature, *Man is not a Bird* (1966) uses
cross-cutting and juxtaposition to expand the simple love story
between a young woman and an older man into a complex
picture of life. His most famous film is his second feature, *Love
Dossier—Tragedy of a Switchboard Operator* (1967). Makavejev's technique, which has, of course, been compared to that of
Godard, approaches the collage: interviews, stills, clips from

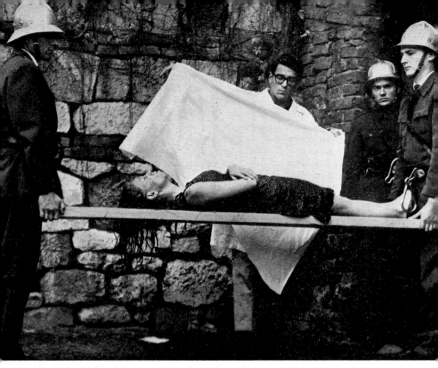

Dušan Makavejev's *Tragedy of a Switchboard Operator* (1967)

documentaries are woven into the story of a love affair between Isabella, a young switchboard operator, and an older man, Ahmed the rat-catcher. The film opens with an illustrated lecture by a sexologist, then, after the titles, cuts to Isabella and rapidly, with little explanation, shows her meeting with Ahmed. There follows a sudden and unexplained cut to a dark well from which the body of a girl is removed. This leads into a lecture on murder before abruptly cutting back to the hero and heroine. In fact the cut to the body of the girl is a flash forward, and the film proceeds, continuing the process of juxtaposition, to unfold the events leading to

Ruzica Sokic, Eva Ras in Makavejev's *Tragedy of a Switchboard Operator*

the 'tragedy of the switchboard operator'. The effect of these
techniques is to create irony—the distancing of the spectator,
preventing him from becoming too emotionally involved with the
film—and to establish different perspectives. One has a general
comment on sexuality and a clinical presentation of assassination,
which are illustrated, on the human, individual level, by the story
of Ahmed and Isabella. At the same time Makavejev can be seen
questioning the socialist revolution. The scenes showing political
banners and posters are inter-cut with sequences of the heroine
walking through the streets; the lack of relation between the two

emphasizes the underlying thesis that despite structural changes in society the emotional and especially sexual problems between individuals remain unresolved. And is it not with the individual that Makavejev ultimately sympathizes? Is this not the effect of the final image—where, although Isabella is dead and Ahmed arrested, the two are shown, in long shot, walking down the steps, in front of the apartment house where they lived?

Makavejev's next film, *Innocence Unprotected* (1968), could be described as a form of documentary; the title refers to the first Serbian talkie, which was made in 1942 during the Nazi occupation. Makavejev has, however, created a work which very much bears his trademark. Using clips from the original film, documentary material from the period and modern interviews with the director and actors of the first *Innocence Unprotected,* Makavejev gives us once again a complex collage. Aleksić, the director of the original film, was a stuntman and although now maimed by an accident, he is still naïvely proud of his strength. His own film is ludicrously bad and the simple virtues it expresses are put in ironic perspective by clips from contemporary material about the occupation. While the effect is often to poke fun at Aleksić, the film as a whole views him with a form of ironic affection.

In this montage Makavejev's attitudes to the individual and to life itself are again revealed. 'His films,' said Robin Wood in *Second Wave*, 'suggest that truth, if it exists at all, is many-sided, and composed of an elaborate complex of contradictions.'

Judging from the few films that have found distributors in the West, the Yugoslavian cinema has fostered some extremely distinctive and stylistically varied directors. This is not very astonishing, perhaps, for a country which is divided into six republics, has five languages and four religions. Yet most of the films from Yugoslavia are characterized by a concern for the individual, with all his weaknesses, and an often highly critical portrayal of society. This can be seen by the choice and treatment of characters who are often semi-criminal and quite the opposite of the 'positive' hero of socialist realism.

Dušan Makavejev's *Innocence Unprotected* (1968) ▶

Albania, Romania,
the German Democratic Republic, Bulgaria

As yet nothing has emerged from Albania that could be remotely considered as 'new cinema'. Romania has produced some interesting cartoons but in the field of the feature film there has been little of importance, despite a number of co-productions with other countries. In 1970, however, *The Reconstruction*, directed by Lucian Pintilie, was praised during the Directors' Fortnight at Cannes; the film has a contemporary setting and takes a fairly critical attitude towards the state.

In the GDR the documentary has flourished, especially through the efforts of Andrew and Anneliese Thorndike, but in the realm of the feature there is no real sign of a New Wave.

Joachim Kunert's *The Adventures of Werner Holt* (1964)

Sasha Krusharka in Konrad Wolf's *Stars* (1959)

Among the few films that have received praise abroad are *The Adventures of Werner Holt* (1964), directed by Joachim Kunert, and *Stars* (1959), directed by Konrad Wolf. The first of these films deals with the events leading up to the end of the Second World War. Through a series of flashbacks while the hero waits for battle, the director shows Werner Holt coming to a realization of the truth about Nazism.

Stars is also set in the Second World War and again deals with a man's discovery of the true implications of fascism. By falling in love with a Jewess, Ruth, confined in a camp in Bulgaria before being sent on to Dachau or Auschwitz, a German sergeant comes to realize that he too bears a responsibility for the atrocities committed by his government. At the time when it was made the film was unusual in its sensitive portrayal of the German officer.

Stars was a co-production with Bulgaria which has recently shown signs of the growth of an interesting 'new cinema'. Among its feature directors known abroad is Rangel Vulchanov who began making features in the late fifties. In 1962 he directed *Sun and Shadow* which was fairly widely shown outside Bulgaria. Set in a seaside holiday resort, the film shows the meeting between a Bulgarian boy and a girl from the West. As they grow fond of each other, they become concerned with the possibility of a nuclear war. Thus their personal situation makes them reflect on questions concerning mankind as a whole. The film is unfortunately rather naïve and the imaginary sequence of an atomic disaster is poorly shot, but the work is distinguished by its non-partisan condemnation of war.

War is also condemned, but much more subtly, in the films of Vulo Radev, Bulgaria's most distinguished director. His first feature, *The Peach Thief* (1964), is set in the last months of the First World War in a small Bulgarian town which houses a prisoner-of-war camp. With the end of hostilities in sight, the prisoners enjoy a certain amount of freedom. Ivo, a young Serbian officer, succeeds in slipping past the camp guards and steals some peaches from the garden of the elderly town commandant, but is caught red-handed by the latter's young wife, Lisa. The film shows the gradual development of their love which ends tragically with the death of the Serbian : while his fellow prisoners are being evacuated he slips away to rejoin Lisa but is shot by the commandant's orderly who has orders to fire on thieves stealing peaches from the garden. The relationship between these two

on pages 146–7
George Naoumov, Anna Prutsnal in Ranghel Vulchanov's *Sun and Shadow* (1962)

Rade Marković, Nevena Kokanova in Vulo Radev's *The Peach Thief* (1964)

Radev's *The Peach Thief*

Nevena Kokanova, Victor Rebenchuk in Vulo Radev's *The Longest Night* (1969) ▶

'enemies' is seen as something positive, although doomed, against the background of war, which maims, brutalizes and destroys. Impeccably acted by Nevena Kokanova as Lisa and Rade Marković as Ivo, *The Peach Thief* is an extremely moving film distinguished by its beautifully composed shots and its skilful evocation of period atmosphere.

In *The Longest Night* (1969)—again starring Nevena Kokanova —Vulo Radev turns to the Second World War. Hunted by the Germans and the Bulgarian police, a British airman hides in a train travelling through the night to Sofia. The long journey is of course a standard dramatic situation whereby very different characters can be brought together and observed as they react to a common danger. The film shows the initial fears and hesitations of the passengers but gradually a feeling of solidarity grows up between them until these ordinary people are willing to endanger themselves in order to save the fugitive.

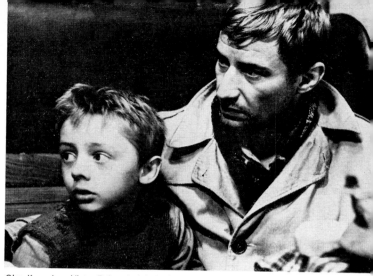

Oleg Kovachev, Victor Rebenchuk in Radev's *The Longest Night*

◀ Dimiter Tashev in *Ikonostasis* (1969) directed by Todor Dinov and Hristo Hristov

Thus once again Radev's humanism is in evidence:

I was attracted by the possibility of reproducing again the theme started with *The Peach Thief* . . . about the inner protest against the senselessness of war, about the human element in man and faith in him, about the solidarity of man against contemporary nihilism, about what it means to serve others wholeheartedly.

However, despite fine performances by the actors, the characters appear very stereotyped. And the ironic conclusion, meant as an indictment of war in general, clashes with the conventional heroics of the rest of the film—nemesis-like, a sudden air-raid apparently destroys the fugitive, thereby cancelling out all the sacrifices that have been made. Nevertheless, Radev's intentions are praiseworthy and *The Longest Night* is fairly entertaining, although it lacks the subtlety of the director's first film.

If Vulo Radev was the first feature director from Bulgaria to be acclaimed abroad, Todor Dinov was his counterpart in the field of animation. The latter has since turned to live-action films and together with Hristo Hristov directed a first feature, *Ikonostasis* (1969). This is adapted from a famous novel about Bulgaria's attempts to break away from the Ottoman empire. The two directors have not attempted a faithful adaptation but have drawn

Sidetracked (1967) directed by Grisha Ostrovski and Todor Stoyanov

freely from the original novel. Their intention was not to make a carefully documented historical film. As Hristov said, 'I believe there is no sense in producing historical films unless we find the problems of our own times reflected there.'

The hero of the film is a master woodcarver, an artist trying to create new values and seeking liberty from the narrow-minded, reactionary society that surrounds him. By concentrating on the problems of liberty, revolution and the rôle of the artist in society the directors have made a film which can appeal to a wide audience despite its specifically Bulgarian setting. At the same time there is a great feeling for plastic beauty revealed in each impeccably composed shot.

Like *Ikonostasis, Sidetracked* (1967) was made by a team of two directors, Grisha Ostrovski and Todor Stoyanov, the gifted cameraman who worked on *The Peach Thief*. This film is concerned with the postwar generation in Bulgaria. A man leaves the

Nevena Kokanova in *Sidetracked*

main road and drives along a 'side track' which he hopes will be a short cut. He comes across an archaeological dig where, to his surprise, he finds a woman he loved seventeen years before. He drives her to town and during the journey they recall and discuss with nostalgia their youthful affair. This is evoked in a manner reminiscent of Alain Resnais through a series of flashbacks which do not present the past in chronological order but fasten on moments of intensity or crisis.

The youth of the immediate postwar years considered love as a diversion—a 'side track'—which should not take precedence over politics or study. It was for this reason that the man and the woman in the film were 'sidetracked' into sacrificing their youthful love. This poetic, sophisticated film, with a title that can be interpreted on many levels, is distinguished by the fine acting of Nevena Kokanova and Ivan Andonov, and by its detached, ironic presentation of the revolutionary spirit of the postwar years.

Stefan Mavrodiev, Kosta Karageorgiev in Georgi Stoyanov's *Birds and Greyhounds* (1969)

Birds and Greyhounds (1969), a first feature by Georgi Stoyanov, is also concerned with youthful revolutionaries but it is a very different work indeed. The setting is a small Bulgarian town during the Second World War, where a group of young resistance fighters are on trial for their lives. This is not, however, a realistic or socialist realist film but a work of fantasy. The director cuts backwards and forwards in time, presents real and imagined events, satirizes the reactionary authorities and mingles high-key poetic sequences with scenes of extreme violence. This extraordinary first feature reveals a film-maker of great imagination who uses fantasy and grotesque black comedy to portray youthful idealism within a corrupt, brutal society.

Birds and Greyhounds, Sidetracked, Ikonostasis show the surprising range of the small but inventive 'new cinema' which emerged in Bulgaria during the 1960s.

Mava Dragomanska in Stoyanov's *Birds and Greyhounds*

Conclusion

The films from the countries discussed in this book do reveal national features: those from Poland appeal to the emotions, use moving symbols and often dwell on images of violence, reflecting the country's romantic tradition; Hungarian films, although mirroring the long history of violent change in their country, appeal much more to the intellect, raise complex socio-political questions and cultivate formal elegance; films from Czechoslovakia can be intimate, brilliantly observed works but are capable of exploiting a vein of disturbing fantasy often reminiscent of Kafka.

There is, however, one recurrent theme—apart from the Second World War—which concerns almost all the Eastern European film-makers: the rôle of the individual in society. This is not, however, treated in the oversimplified manner of socialist realism. Often highly critical of existing social structures, yet aware of the complexity of the problems of individual and collective responsibility, these directors have created a 'new cinema' in Eastern Europe distinguished not only by its formal experiments but by its profound examination of fundamental problems of human existence.

Acknowledgements

I should like to thank the following organizations for supplying the stills reproduced: Avala Films, British Film Institute, Central Booking Agency, Connoisseur Films, Contemporary Films, Educational and Television Films, FRZ (Belgrade), Filmbulgaria, Film Polski, Hungarofilm, Hunter Films and the Darville Organization, National Film Archive, Planet Films, Twentieth-Century Fox.

Warm thanks to Charles Hedges for his invaluable help in gathering photographs and information, and to David Bindman, Stanley Forman, Martin Heath, Josephine Hickey, Tom Mabbett, Colin McArthur, Angela Rose, Lotte Steinhart and all the staff of Contemporary Films.

Bibliography

L'avant scène du cinéma no. 47 (special issue on Poland). Paris, April 1965

Eastern Europe by Nina Hibbins. London: Zwemmer 1970; New York: Barnes 1970

Image et Son no. 217, May 1968

International Film Guide edited by Peter Cowie. London: The Tantivy Press; New York: Barnes, published yearly

Jeune cinéma hongrois by Claude B. Levenson. Premier Plan no. 43. Lyon: SERDOC 1966.

Jeune cinéma tchecoslovaque by Marie-Magdeleine Brumagne. Premier Plan no. 52. Lyon: SERDOC 1969

Andrzej Munk by J. Plazewsky. Paris: Anthologie du cinéma 1967

Nouveaux cinéastes polonais by Philippe Haudiquet. Premier Plan no. 27. Lyon: SERDOC 1963.

Second Wave a symposium. London: Studio Vista 1970; New York: Praeger 1970

Andrzej Wajda by Hadelin Trinon. Cinéma d'aujourd'hui no. 26. Paris: Seghers 1964

Andrzej Wajda: Polish cinema edited by Colin McArthur, A BFI Education Department Dossier, December 1970

Index